SET SAIL

YOUR GUIDE TO MEAL PLANNING, PROVISIONING, AND BOAT-FRIENDLY RECIPES FOR CHARTER YACHT VACATIONS

NEVENA MRDALJ

**SET SAIL: Your Guide to Meal Planning,
Provisioning, and Boat-Friendly Recipes for Charter Yacht Vacations**

Text and Photographs © 2025 by Nevena Mrdalj

Published by Nevena M. Mrdalj

ISBN: 979-8-218-62341-8

First Edition: March 2025
Printed in The United States of America
Cover design by Srdjan Stojicic
Interior design by Dawn Black
Photography by Nevena Mrdalj
Photo Advisor: Janise Witt
Editor: Katie Benoit
Proofreader: Rob Bignell, Inventing Reality Editing Service
Printed and distributed by Acutrack, Inc

Disclaimer: While every effort has been made to ensure the accuracy of the recipes and safety tips included, the author and publisher are not responsible for any accidents, injuries, or mishaps that may occur while cooking onboard. Always follow proper boating and fire safety guidelines.

For more information, tips, and updates, visit: **SetSailCookbook.com**

CONTENTS

INTRODUCTION   8

PART ONE:

MEAL PLANNING AND PROVISIONING

CHAPTER 1: SET REALISTIC EXPECTATIONS   17

CHAPTER 2: GATHER INPUT AND PLAN ITINERARY   23

CHAPTER 3: HOW TO MAKE A MEAL PLAN   29

CHAPTER 4: PROVISIONING YOUR BOAT   41

CHAPTER 5: BEFORE YOU LEAVE THE MARINA   63

PART TWO:

BOAT-FRIENDLY RECIPES

CHAPTER 6: BEVERAGES   77

THE JVD COCKTAIL   82

THE BVI PAINKILLER   83

RUM PASSION   84

TING WITH A STING   85

TROPICAL SEABREEZE (NA)   86

GUAVA SPRITZER (NA)   87

PASSION FANTASY (NA)   88

THE DRY TONIC (NA)   89

CHAPTER 7: BREAKFAST FOODS   91

OVERNIGHT OATS   93

PEANUT BUTTER BANANA WRAP   94

AVOCADO TOAST 95

CITRUS SALAD 96

QUINOA CUP 97

YOGURT BERRY PARFAIT 98

MANGO BANANA SMOOTHIE 99

BERRY PASSION SMOOTHIE 100

GREEN ENERGY BOOST SMOOTHIE 101

PAPAYA SMOOTHIE 102

SOURSOP PINEAPPLE SMOOTHIE 103

STRAWBERRY YOGURT SMOOTHIE 104

MEDITERRANEAN EGGWHITES 105

EGG BREAKFAST BURRITO 106

BREAKFAST SKILLETS 107

TOFU SCRAMBLE 108

POACHED EGG AND AVOCADO 109

CHAPTER 8: SNACKS AND APPETIZERS 111

MEXICAN DIP 112

HUMMUS AND VEGGIES 113

EGGS WITH SMOKED SALMON 114

CELERY WITH BOURSIN 115

SHRIMP COCKTAIL 116

CHEESE AND CUCUMBER BITES 117

MEZZE PLATTER 118

CHAPTER 9: SANDWICHES AND SOUPS 121

HAM AND CHEESE SANDWICH 122

TURKEY AVOCADO POCKET 123

TUNA SALAD 124

VEGGIE WRAP 125

LOX BAGEL 126

EGG SALAD 127

QUESADILLA 128

AVOCADO SOUP 129

GAZPACHO 130

CHAPTER 10: COLD DISHES 133

CHICKEN WALDORF SALAD 134

ANTIPASTO SALAD 136

PINEAPPLE CHICKEN SLAW 138

CAJUN SHRIMP 140

TUNA AND WHITE BEAN SALAD 142

SHRIMP AND AVOCADO SALAD 144

DEVILED SHRIMP 146

ANEGADA LOBSTER SALAD 148

NICOISE SALAD 150

TUNA WITH GREEN BEANS 152

CARIBBEAN QUINOA SALAD 154

BLACK BEAN SALAD 156

LENTIL SALAD 158

VEGGIE PASTA SALAD 160

RAMEN NOODLE SALAD 162

CHICKPEA MACARONI SALAD 164

MIXED BEAN SALAD 166

CHAPTER 11: FROM THE STOVETOP 169

JERK CHICKEN FAJITAS 170

PASTA WITH MEATBALLS 172

PAN-SEARED CHICKEN 174

PESTO SHRIMP 176

LENTIL BOLOGNESE 178

ARTICHOKE PASTA 180

WHITE BEANS AND SPINACH 182

CHAPTER 12: FROM THE GRILL 185

BURGERS 186

STEAK 188

GRILLED CHICKEN BREAST 190

HERBED PORK TENDERLOIN 192

HOT DOGS AND SAUSAGES 194

PITA PIZZAS 196

COCONUT SHRIMP 198

MAHI-MAHI WITH SALSA VERDE 200

RED SNAPPER WITH MANGO SALSA 202

SEASONED SALMON 204

GRILLED TOFU WITH CHIMICHURRI 206

CAULIFLOWER STEAK 208

CHAPTER 13: EASY SIDES 211

ADRIATIC POTATO SALAD 212

SPICY CORN 214

QUINOA 215

FRENCH GREEN BEANS 216

SPAGHETTI SQUASH NOODLES 217

MEDITERRANEAN SALAD 218

SPINACH WITH BOURSIN 220

GRILLED VEGGIES 222

CHAPTER 14: SWEET ENDINGS 225

AVOCADO CHOCOLATE MOUSSE 226

PINEAPPLE CHIA PUDDING 227

COOL APPLE COMPOTE 228

MANGO MOUSSE 230

COCONUT CHOCOLATE PUDDING 232

GRILLED PINEAPPLE 234

APPENDIX	239
CONVERSIONS AND EQUIVALENTS	239
COMMON PACKAGE SIZES AND NUMBER OF SERVINGS	241
CHECKLISTS AND NOTES	242
ACKNOWLEDGMENTS	246
ABOUT THE AUTHOR	249

INTRODUCTION

Are you excited about your upcoming charter yacht vacation?

When my husband and I and some friends booked our first bare-boat yacht in the Virgin Islands about ten years ago, we couldn't wait to go. We received some brochures and maps from our charter broker, and we kept looking at the pictures of beautiful boats, blue water, palm trees, and sandy beaches. We had been on many vacations but had never vacationed on a yacht. Our focus for this new adventure was on what types of water activities we wanted to do, which islands to see, and which restaurants to try. We couldn't wait to leave for our vacation and spend time with our friends sailing, snorkeling, swimming, and, of course, enjoying delicious meals and cocktails in a magical setting.

We glanced at the mention of provisioning in the charter's welcome letter when we booked the trip, but we didn't really give it much thought until just a couple of weeks before our trip. That's when we learned that provisioning a bareboat yacht means bringing on board everything you need for your vacation. We were all set with bathing suits, floaties, and sunscreen, but when we started thinking about food, that was another story. Looking at the description of the boat's refrigerator, we realized that it seemed very small and the freezer even smaller—at least compared to our appliances at home. We wondered how and where we would store our food and what we could prepare in that small kitchen space.

You may be asking the same questions.

It turns out that provisioning a bareboat charter yacht for a group of people is a challenging task, and most articles and blogs leave out the details you need to carefully plan. We found ourselves struggling to get prepared, and so our first charter yacht vacation was rocky, not only because of the waves but because there was so much that we did not know about boating, provisioning, and preparing meals while on board. Just like with any other event, the smallest of details can make or break an experience. Our expectations were high, since this was a vacation that we had been looking forward to for a long time.

Since that first rocky trip, I have learned a lot about meal planning for a whole week and provisioning a yacht for a group of people—who often have different dietary needs and tastes. Over the last decade I have prepared for more than twenty charter yacht trips and spent more than fifty weeks on a bareboat charter—not as a chef but as someone who is there on vacation, just like you. Most of our time has been spent in the Virgin Islands, but we have also cruised in Puerto Rico, the Bahamas, Canada, and the South of France. We have vacationed on a boat with family and friends and by ourselves. And while each trip offered up a unique combination of people, age groups, and dietary preferences, the preparation and provisioning process was the same for all trips, and certain tips while aboard a boat or yacht apply universally as well.

We have come to love vacationing on boats and know you will, too. Picture this—the perfect day: We find ourselves sipping on cocktails while watching the sun slowly sink into the horizon. When the surface of the sea has become smooth like a mirror, the still water has a calming effect. We prepared dinner earlier in the day; the cold shrimp marinating in the refrigerator will taste delicious with the veggie pasta salad after a day in the sun. We have the whole evening in front of us and will eat whenever we feel like it, finishing the meal off with mango mousse under the stars. The perfect day indeed.

With all these boat charters under my belt, I realized a couple of years ago that I had finally gotten the hang of how to plan for a bareboat charter trip and that my planning steps, menu lists, grocery lists, and boat-friendly recipes and food ideas could be useful to others. As I reviewed my recipes, I realized that most had connections to the Mediterranean Sea, and now I had some new additions from the Caribbean Sea. What started off as quick notes I jotted down on each journey turned into this book, full of tips and lessons I had learned over time.

It also features realistic meals that we prepared regularly on our boat vacations using only common ingredients that are easily obtained almost anywhere.

This guide is for those planning a vacation on a bareboat yacht with family or friends usually in groups of four to eight people. I will walk you through the complete process of provisioning your boat with food and beverages, starting with which questions to ask and which details to think about once you charter a bareboat. I will help you plan meals, quantities, and types of foods. The recipes I present here cater to modern tastes and take into account common dietary restrictions and preferences, such as gluten-free, dairy-free, vegan, and vegetarian options. These recipes feature mostly classic American and Mediterranean dishes, some with a Caribbean influence.

This book will:

- Provide you with an overview of the limitations and possibilities of living aboard a yacht while on a Caribbean vacation.
- Aid you in reducing the stress of the unknown.
- Guide you through a logical step-by-step planning process for a bareboat charter vacation.
- Give you boat-friendly and delicious recipes and ideas that are quick, easy, and foolproof.
- Teach you how to accommodate group members with dietary restrictions.
- Help you put together a meal plan quickly because the recipes are marked with common dietary labels.
- Give you checklists, suggested shopping lists, and provisioning tips.
- Save you lots of time and money while also reducing food waste.
- Increase the chances that everyone on board will have a wonderful vacation.

Through trial and error, I have found the recipes presented here to be easy to prepare and to taste good on a boat in the tropical climate. I have learned many lessons about food, fun, knots, and yachts over the last decade. Now I am passing the lessons surrounding food on to you.

I hope this guide will help you plan and prepare for a fabulous vacation on your charter yacht.

Smooth sailing!

Nevena Mrdalj
Certified Skipper and Dinghy Cap'n

NEVENA MRDALJ

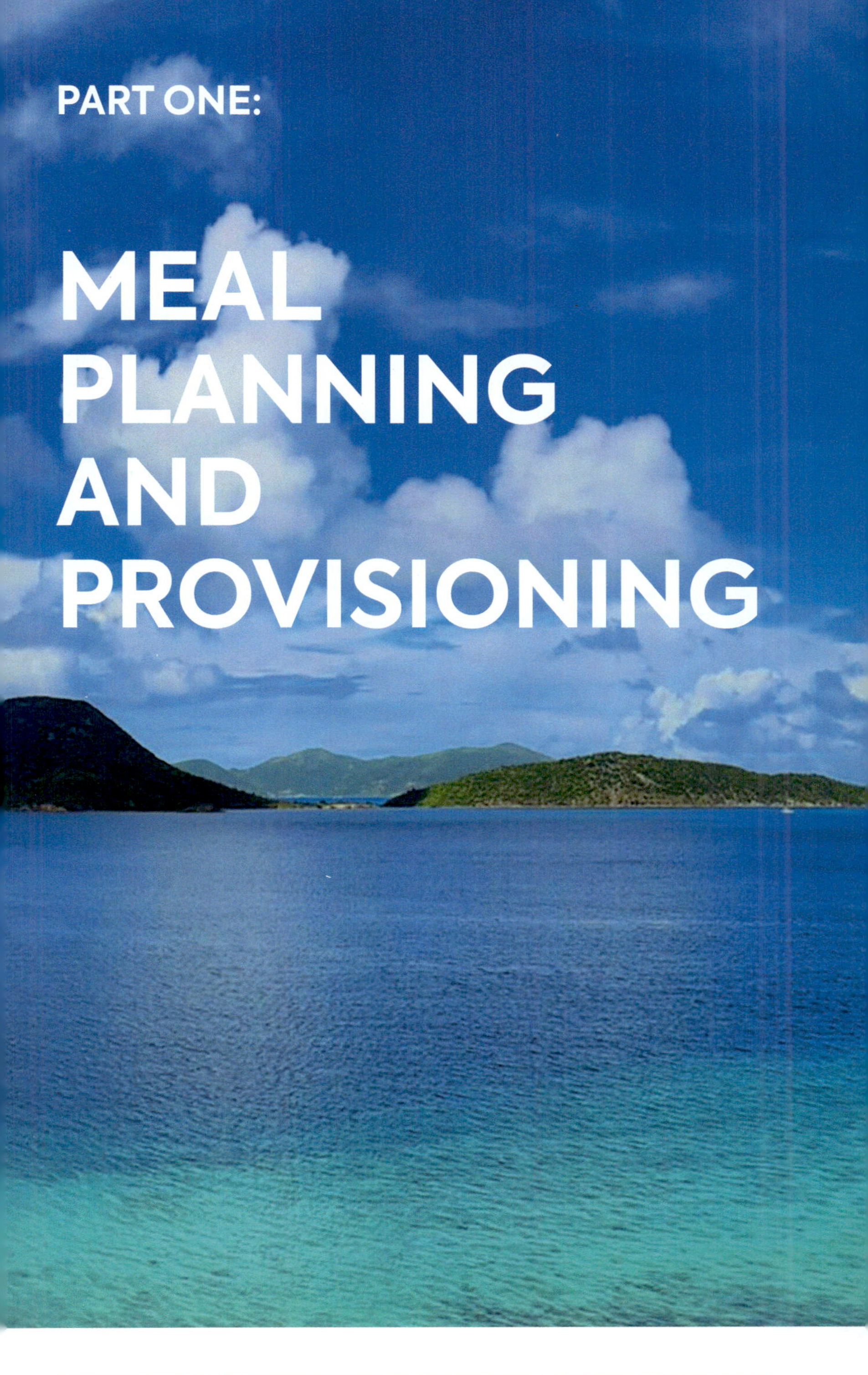

MEAL PLANNING AND PROVISIONING

There are many aspects to planning a bareboat charter vacation. A bareboat is a chartered boat or yacht that is "bare" of a crew and provisions meaning that you are responsible for captaining yourself or hiring a captain, buying groceries and preparing meals. However, most advertisements are focused on all-inclusive charters; those images with chefs and fancy meal presentations may influence your expectations, which are not in line with the bareboat experience and reality. That is not to say that your meals will not be enjoyable. The lush islands and the turquoise water will be the same for all. The panoramic views and golden sunsets transform any ordinary meal into a memorable experience, making even simple foods taste better. The difference is that on a bareboat everyone will have to participate in the food preparation, requiring you to have simple and foolproof recipes.

Most of the yachts chartered in the Caribbean are bareboats because they are much more affordable than all-inclusive charters. Many books and blogs explain the ins and outs of navigating around the islands in a charter yacht and what you need to know if you plan to captain the boat yourself. This guide focuses specifically on food—and everything related to food. Because the British Virgin Islands (BVI) are one of the most popular destinations for first-time bareboat charterers, I will illustrate the food planning and provisioning process using BVI stores and locations.

CHAPTER 1

SET REALISTIC EXPECTATIONS

A bareboat yacht is usually very comfortable and comes with an equipped kitchen (called the galley) and cabins stocked with towels and linens. It has a generator, and often there is air conditioning as well. You can hire a captain or sail the boat yourself if you have experience. Either way, on a bareboat you plan out your own itinerary, rent your water toys, pay for fuel and the mooring fees, and prepare your own meals and drinks. The atmosphere on a bareboat is more intimate, and you will have options to dine in restaurants or aboard. Since food and drink are an especially important part of how we experience any vacation, you will need to provision your boat with everything you and your group need before you set sail. Don't forget that you are also responsible for meals for your hired captain. Before your trip and before you make your grocery list, open and honest communication will be very important so that everyone has on board the types of food and drink that they like; remember, there are no grocery stores just around the corner. Each guest needs to have a clear picture of what to expect.

Understand the Limitations of Boat Living

Yacht life is wonderful, but it's a completely different experience than land living, even for the most basic and smallest of details. When provisioning your yacht, you'll have to account for the differences that come with this type of vacation. Here are the most common limitations of living and cooking on a boat:

- You need to buy water for drinking—and for cooking.
- Your refrigerator may be as big as a regular oven, and your freezer may be the size of a full-size microwave oven.
- Beverages are kept in chest coolers, which you need to replenish with ice daily.
- You have a limited number of pots and pans, dishes, and utensils.
- There often is no dishwasher and only a very small sink.
- The stovetop may not be able to accommodate two large pots or pans at once.
- An oven, if used, will heat the galley and the cabins of the boat.
- You cannot and should not prepare food while underway.
- You may need to run the generator for some meal preparations.

About Food and Essentials

Many cookbooks for boaters claim and demonstrate that you can cook at home on a boat just about anything that you can cook at home. While this is true if you have only two or three people aboard and if you spend several weeks or months sailing, on a one-week vacation with a group of six to eight people, you need to consider not only the ingredients for a particular meal but also clean-up time. And you might find yourself adapting your at-home recipes for on the boat. Let me give you an example.

Bacon and eggs are an all-American breakfast combination, and bacon is mentioned on many provisioning lists. However, according to several charter companies, bacon is the number one food item left behind on charter yachts—and usually there is a lot of bacon. When I first heard this, I was surprised. But after we made bacon and eggs one morning for six people, I fully understood why. The grease splattered not just all over the cooktop but also onto the blender, toaster and the knife set. Even the floor was greasy and became slippery—not ideal when you are barefoot on a boat. It was difficult to clean up, and the cooking process took a while. We also had one member of our group complain about the lingering smell. That was the last time we cooked bacon while on a sailing vacation. I think that most charterers are like us—they cook bacon once and decide it is not worth the trouble. So, I adapted our at-home recipes; for on-boat recipes that require bacon, bacon bits are the answer.

Ease of preparation, storage requirements, types of kitchen appliances and clean-up time are all factors that play a role in what you will choose to eat. Prepared frozen meals are available for purchase, but lack of freezer space is a major drawback. Check out the recommendations for storing various foods aboard in Chapter 4 (page 41) before you make your meal plans and grocery lists.

On any boat, water is a major resource, and everyone needs to be mindful of how much they have. You only have as much water as is in your water tanks. Those tanks are refilled either at fuel docks, where you can purchase water, or by a water maker, if your boat is equipped with one. The water maker basically removes the salt from the sea water, and you have "fresh" water. That water is used for showering, washing dishes, and flushing toilets (called heads). Bottled water is recommended for cooking and drinking.

You also need to keep an eye on ice for your chest coolers. You need to keep your beverages cold. Ice melts quickly in the tropics, and you will need to replenish it daily. Ice is sold at fuel docks and grocery stores. But the most convenient way to buy ice is from locals who will stop by your yacht with their small boats and offer to sell you bags of ice and take your trash for a fee. Other boats may offer freshly baked goods or collect mooring fees. All these transactions require cash on hand. (See "What to Bring from Home" on page 56.)

How is Your Yacht Equipped?

When you book your vacation, you will charter a certain type of a boat or yacht. Refrigerators, freezers, stoves, and grills often vary in size and type from one boat to another, depending on the size and layout of the boat. However, charter companies usually provide the same small kitchen appliances and accessories for their whole fleet. Find out more details about what your boat will have on board. This will allow you to better plan the types of meals you will prepare. For example, an electric grill heats up quickly, and you can start cooking shortly before you want to eat. On the other hand, a charcoal grill will take some time to preheat. Here are some things to consider when reviewing the kitchen accessories available.

- How many and what types of refrigerators and freezers are included? How big are they?
- Is there a grill? What type is it—charcoal, propane, or electric? How much grilling surface is there? Can it grill all the burgers/fish/chicken at once or will it need two or more rounds? How long will it take for the grill grates to get hot?
- How many chest coolers are aboard for soda, beer, water, and juice? Does it have a three- to five-gallon jug for storing cold drinking water and refilling personal water bottles?
- Is there a microwave?
- What type of stove is it, and how many stovetop burners are there? Is there an oven?
- What type of coffee maker is there? What types of filters does it need? Are the filters provided by the charter company or do we need to buy/bring our own?
- Is there a blender?
- Is there a toaster, and how many slices of bread can it fit?
- Are there any other kitchen appliances?
- How many pots and pans, food containers with lids, cutting boards, kitchen knives, measuring cups, and serving utensils, etc. are provided?

Knowing what you can expect to find in the kitchen will help you to better plan your meals. While thinking about foods seems mundane and boring, food is very important, especially on a bareboat yacht. But before we jump into meal planning, first we need to talk about what your group's adventures will look like.

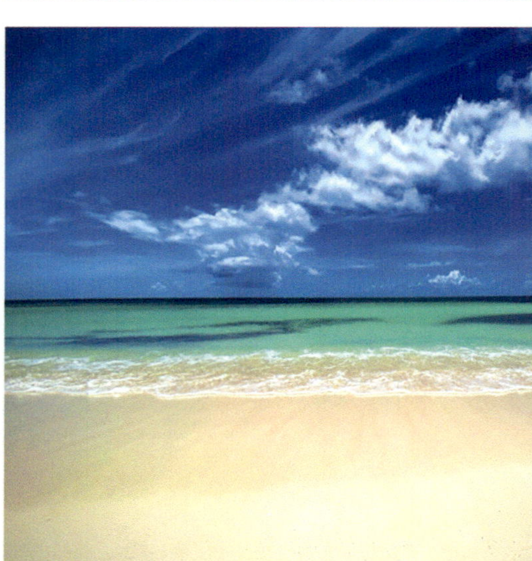

CHAPTER 2

GATHER INPUT AND PLAN ITINERARY

You are dreaming of having a whole beach to yourself, beachcombing and swimming with baby turtles, while your friends are researching good diving spots and looking into kiteboarding. You probably can't wait to leave for the islands and experience this new yacht vacation adventure. We'll get you to that quiet beach and those turquoise waters soon, but not before you complete the preparation process, which may take a bit longer than you think. It is a good idea to start preparing a couple of months before your trip. As you will see, there are a lot of decisions to be made by the group as a whole, and some of the decisions will require information-gathering beforehand. But you can make the process fun! Host a dinner night with your group to try out some cocktails and do a potluck with recipes from this book and a discussion about activities. You can even do some of that virtually if your group is scattered over a large geographical area.

Making last-minute decisions regarding food does not work when you are on a charter yacht. Planning meals for a group of people has its challenges, but it is well worth the effort, considering that groceries are expensive. Determining ahead of time your meal plans—including visiting restaurants, if desired—is something that needs the entire group's signoff. Lots of communication beforehand is key. Here are six things that you need to consider and talk about with your group:

What Type of Vacation is This?

When you started booking your yacht charter, your group members probably had ideas of how they envisioned this vacation. Identifying the "type" of vacation you want—relaxing under the sun around the boat or hitting up the popular hot spots, for example—helps you map out a rough schedule for your trip that can then anchor your meal planning itinerary. Is this a family vacation with different age groups, or is this a vacation with a group of friends? Will your goal be to get in as much sailing as possible or to relax as much as possible? Do you want to go where you can party or have the whole beach to yourself? Do people want a lot of water activities around the boat and, therefore, eat lunch on it, or do you want to visit all the bars to find out which one makes the best Painkiller cocktail and have lunch ashore? Will you start sailing at the crack of dawn, or will you have a leisurely breakfast first?

Where Do You Want to Go?

Your charter company may give you a recommended route/itinerary for your length of stay, complete with sailing distances. Taking the suggestions from the charter company into account, as well as the discussion and input from above, your group should compile a list of activities everyone wants to do (ashore and around the boat), beaches and islands to visit, and local restaurants to try.

What is Your Budget?

Budgetary constraints also need to be taken into consideration. Eating aboard the boat usually is significantly less expensive than eating in restaurants. Food on the islands is always more expensive than on the U.S. mainland. In 2024 in the British Virgin Islands, the groceries for the recipes outlined in this guide were a little less than $200 per person for seven days and included seven breakfasts, eight lunches/dinners, snacks, soft drinks, and water. This amount excluded alcoholic beverages.

Do You Want to Eat Meals Aboard?

Your group may decide that you will eat as many meals as possible in restaurants. That becomes your food plan. It will require that you plan your itinerary and route so that you are near a restaurant for meal-times. Often that is possible.

On the other hand, your group may also decide that preparing food and eating aboard in a relaxed and intimate setting will be more memorable. They don't mind cooking a meal while sipping on a cock-tail. Having food on board also gives you complete freedom to change your itinerary at any time. How many meals (and which ones) would you like to prepare as a group on your yacht?

Often, people will pick something between these two scenarios.

Who is Willing to Help with Meals?

The answer to this question needs to be "most of the people in the group" so that the burden of cooking does not fall on any one person. The recipes in this book are designed to involve everyone so that it takes less than thirty minutes to prepare any one meal. If only one or two people want to be involved, pick more restaurants to go to.

Preparing a simple meal while watching the sun dipping into the sea, the pelicans gliding above you in the sky, and the sea turtles pop-ping their heads out of the water can be fun. There is a job for everyone: grilling meat or fish, chopping vegetables, boiling water for pasta, opening and draining cans, steaming vegetables in the microwave, setting the table, or washing the dishes after dinner.

Answering all these questions and discussing what people hope to see and do during your vacation is very important. Now that everyone understands the limitations and possibilities of boat galleys, and you know which activities you want to do, the places you want to visit, which restaurants you want to try, and how much time and energy your group wants to put into food preparation, it is time to plan the itinerary.

Plan Your Itinerary

Planning your itinerary is an important step and a big task. Local knowl-edge is very helpful; you can learn a lot from guidebooks, blogs, friends, your charter company, and a local captain, if you have hired one. Your charter company will give you recommendations for routes, fill you in on local weather patterns, and brief you on rules and regulations when you arrive, but much of that information you can gather beforehand as well. You need to combine all the information you have gathered with the activities input from your group. Even though itineraries sometimes need to be adjusted, you should have a general idea of what you will do so you can know what types of meals to make and how much food you will need. Reach an agreement and compromise about your proposed itinerary so that all your crew members are on the same page.

Create a spreadsheet with your itinerary by looking at a map and plugging in the places you want to visit in the order that makes sense or that your charter company recommends for the length of your vacation. First, put down where you will spend the day and where you will stay overnight. Next, list all the types of meals across the top. Then decide when and where you will eat out; highlight those cells, and possibly add the name of the restaurant. It may also be a good idea to know where easily accessible grocery stores are along the way if you want or need to quickly pick up some extra provisions. Let me show you the planning process using popular spots in the British Virgin Islands in the Meals by Day Table (page 27).

The first day of your charter will most likely start in the afternoon, and on the last day you will most likely depart after breakfast. That is why those meals are crossed out. Dinner ashore may be a good idea on the first day, as you are still getting settled. Breakfast on the last day should most likely be something you can eat on the go, as you will be packing to leave. In this particular table, I designated the locations where there is a grocery store with an asterisk (*).

Now you can see exactly how many and what types of meals you need to plan for. For a downloadable "Meals by Day" planning sheet, go to **SetSailCookbook.com**.

	Destination	Breakfast	Lunch	Snack	Dinner	Dessert
Day 1	ARRIVE	x	x			
Night 1	Marina	x	x		R	R
Day 2	Norman					
Night 2	Norman				R	R
Day 3	Jost Van Dyke*		R			
Night 3	Cane Garden *					
Day 4	Guana					
Night 4	Guana					
Day 5	Anegada		R			
Night 5	Anegada				R	R
Day 6	Leverick Bay *					
Night 6	Bitter End				R	R
Day 7	Baths		R			
Night 7	Cooper					
Day 8	DEPART		x	x	x	x

R/highlight=restaurant

X=outside the scope of your trip

*=grocery store with dinghy access

CHAPTER 3

HOW TO MAKE A MEAL PLAN

There are many ways to approach meal planning. It involves a lot of group input and discussion and some compromises to create a plan that will accommodate everyone and each person's dietary needs. When discussing your food preferences with the group, explain why you need to avoid a certain food or eat at a certain time. Giving an explanation will help others understand and be more accommodating. Here are the planning steps I recommend:

See How Many Meals You Need

Looking at the before-mentioned itinerary (see "Meals by Day" table on page 27) as our example, you need to plan for:

- Seven breakfasts
- Seven snacks
- Three lunches
- Three dinners
- Three desserts

There are many easy breakfast options, and most people are used to preparing their own breakfast. The same is true for snacks. This now leaves only six meals to think about and agree on. Desserts are optional.

If you have hired a captain, don't forget to include that person in your group count and planning process.

Itineraries can change for a variety of reasons, so you also want to plan for an extra meal, just in case your schedule changes. Your group may decide to change it. Your charter yacht may need some sort of service. Waiting for the repair technicians to arrive and fix your issue may derail your plans. Sometimes, you cannot get a restaurant reservation. Whatever the reason, it is good to have food for one extra meal on hand just in case. It can be something you would prepare with all canned foods, such as the "Tuna with Green Beans and Tomatoes" meal (page 152) or it could be "Pasta with Meatballs" (page 172). If those food items are left over at the end of the trip, then everything went according to plan, and you leave all unopened food on the yacht on your departure day. The food will be distributed amongst the people working in the marina. But if you end up needing it, you will be glad you had it on hand.

About Allergies and Dietary Preferences

Food allergies and dietary preferences need to be considered. Sometimes the type and severity of someone's dietary restriction will make you lean toward eating aboard, since you have more control over food ingredients.

Allergies can be serious, so ask if someone has an allergy to a particular food (peanuts, shrimp, etc.). I would recommend that you don't have those foods on board. You are in a small environment and accidental exposure can happen easily. It's best to prevent accidents.

Dietary restrictions are very common and can seem complicated and even intimidating when planning meals for a group. If that person is a family member, making the meal plan will seem like second nature, but if it is a friend, then getting input and double checking will be important. The good news is that many foods are suitable for everyone. Those who have food allergies and dietary restrictions should take a close look at the meal suggestions in this book to pick out which meals they can eat and determine if any modifications need to be made to those meals. It is easier for them to read an ingredient list and know immediately if that meal is an option. This is what I call "starting with the lowest common denominator." From there, consider what everyone else likes, as well, and find some overlap. How can you compromise to accommodate everyone? Be flexible in your dish's creation. For example, choose a vegan dish as the base for your "family meal," and then everyone can add cheese, meat, or a different protein according to their liking. Similarly, you can grill one portabella mushroom and five hamburgers and share the same side dishes.

What are the Non-Negotiables for Each Person?

Every person has certain habits when it comes to food. If you are traveling with your family, you may already know the specifics. Even if you do, it is still nice to ask and double check. If you are traveling with friends for the first time, you most likely will not know how they start their day or what they like to have for snacks. Some people associate vacation with a certain drink or food and would like to have that. Don't be shy. Speak up!

In my experience, habits may be something like:

- I like to start my day with coffee.
- I like to have an English muffin and some peanut butter every morning.
- I need eggs for breakfast.
- I need to have three Diet Cokes every day.

Compile a list of everyone's requests, with quantities and details. Everyone should have what they like, if possible. Check online to see if grocery stores stock a needed item. Bring hard-to-find ingredients with you, especially if they are dry and easy to pack. This will eliminate uncertainty since provisioning on islands is less predictable. If bringing a certain food from home is not possible, at least be mentally prepared for what you will have to do without.

Determine Recipe Prep Difficulty

You need to decide how much time and energy you want to expand on cooking meals as a group. How involved do you want meal preparation to be? By now, you may have an idea about the cooking appliances on your yacht, so consider the following questions:

- Do you want to grill? Is the grill surface big enough to grill the main protein for everyone at once? How long will grilling the food take? Be sure to add that time into your itinerary.
- How many people are on the yacht? The more people you have, the simpler your food choices need to be.
- Do you want to use the stovetop? Do you have enough pots and pans for a particular menu plan?
- Does your group find any of the cold meals or salads appealing? They are simpler to prepare because they don't require the use of the generator, stovetop, or grill for the most part.

Choose Recipes

Use this book's recipes for your meal planning. Part Two (page 71) of this book contains many suggestions and more than seventy boat-friendly recipes divided into nine sections (listed below). Look at the categories of interest so you have an idea of what is possible and doable before you continue your discussions and planning process. Each recipe is marked with common dietary labels so that everyone can easily see what appeals to them. See the Dietary Labels Table (page 74) for a description of the labels used in this guide. At the very least, most charterers will need to provision beverages, snacks and some breakfast foods.

- **Beverages**: A wide array, from water and coffee to cocktails and wine.
- **Breakfast Foods**: Many individual preferences in terms of what, when, and how much people like to eat.
- **Snacks and Appetizers**: On a charter yacht vacation, these are mandatory.
- **Sandwiches and Soups**: Easy-to-make middle-of-the-day meals or light entrees.
- **Cold Dishes:** Hearty salads and gourmet meals that are ideal for warm climates.
- **From the Stovetop** : Quick pastas, meats and vegan meals.
- **From the Grill**: American favorites, fish, and vegetables.
- **Easy Sides**: Veggies, starches, and grains.
- **Sweet Endings**: Light and creamy desserts.

As far as meals go, you can choose from the other six categories. Notice that the dishes are grouped by cooking method—cold, stove-top, and grill—for easy reference. Cold dishes need to be chilled and, therefore, require some space in the refrigerator for at least a couple of hours. If your cooktop is electric, you will need to turn on the generator first in order to cook something. If your stove is gas, you will be able to use it without a generator. Grills can be gas, charcoal or electric and models differ from boat to boat. How much time is needed to preheat the grill can vary significantly. I have not included any recipes that require the use of an oven. Ovens need to be preheated and usually take a while to bake the food, all the while generating heat inside the main cabin. In a warm climate, that is not appealing.

It is impossible to categorize all the recipes precisely. For example, pasta salads are cold, but you will need to cook the pasta first at some point—I usually do that in the morning while the generator and air conditioners are still running and I'm waiting for the coffee to brew. Generally, microwaves, coffee makers, toasters, and blenders run on battery power, and you can use them at any time. Just like at home, this makes grabbing a quick bite or preparing a dish easy and flexible for planning.

When discussing recipes or food ideas, it is a good idea to get very specific feedback from everyone. "I do like this, but I don't like that." Or "I can eat this, but I can't eat that." The one answer that you should not accept from anyone is: "Don't worry about me—I am easy. I can just have X." Well, on a boat, you need to have "X" on hand—that is the whole point of planning ahead. Often, those who wait until they have arrived on the yacht to say they don't eat a particular food are the same people who did not put in the required time to consider boat limitations and communicate with the group.

Make your Meal Plan

Looking at your itinerary, designate when you plan on preparing each specific meal. You may not end up eating each meal in that order, but it is helpful to have your selections penciled in. As you look at the day's meal plan, you will see that, for example, you plan to have chicken breasts that evening, which means that you will need to take out the chicken to defrost a few hours beforehand. If you plan to grill that evening, it means that you need to be back on the boat by a certain time. If you are going to snorkel mid-morning and you want to have a pasta salad for lunch, it means that you will need to make the salad in the morning so it will be ready to eat when everyone gets back to the boat.

Cook once—eat twice! For example, if you plan on grilling for dinner, you can grill extra chicken breasts and have them with a salad the next day. If you make a hearty salad as a side for dinner, you can eat the leftovers for lunch the next day. If you plan on grilling or sauteing vegetables, you may want to do that at the beginning of your vacation. When cooked, those vegetables will take up a lot less refrigerator space and will keep for up to five days to be incorporated into other meals and snacks.

Once you put together the menu for the week, make sure people who follow specific diets review the selections and the ingredients listed one more time to make sure they will be able to eat the group meals. If any compromises need to be made, it is best to have hard conversations before your trip so that everyone has time to process the information, and you avoid flaring tempers while in confined quarters.

The Sample Meal Plan (page 35) illustrates what a weekly meal plan could look like for the previously planned itinerary (page 27). In the breakfast and snack columns, two options are given.

Sample Meal Plan

	Destination	Breakfast	Lunch	Snack	Dinner	Dessert
Day 1	ARRIVE	x	x	chips, salsa & guacamole		
Night 1	Marina	x	x	cheese & crackers	RESTAURANT	RESTAURANT
Day 2	Norman	1-Egg Breakfast Burrito 2-Green Energy Smoothie	sandwiches	pretzels		
Night 2	Norman			Celery with Boursin	RESTAURANT	RESTAURANT
Day 3	Jost Van Dyke *	1-Overnight Oats 2-Berry Passion Smoothie	RESTAURANT	mixed nuts		
Night 3	Cane Garden *			Mexican Dip	Red Snapper with Mango Salsa & Rice	Grilled Pineapple
Day 4	Guana	1-Poached Egg & Avocado 2-Papaya Smoothie	Antipasto Salad	popcorn		
Night 4	Guana			Eggs with Smoked Salmon	Cajun Shrimp & Veggie Pasta Salad	Mango Mousse
Day 5	Anegada	1-PB Banana Wrap 2-Strawberry Yogurt Smoothie	RESTAURANT	Cheese & Cucumber Bites		
Night 5	Anegada			Shrimp Cocktail	RESTAURANT	RESTAURANT
Day 6	Leverick Bay *	1-Mediterranean Egg Whites 2-Mango Banana Smoothie	Gazpacho & Quesadillas	Hummus and Veggies		
Night 6	Bitter End			Mezze Platter	RESTAURANT	RESTAURANT
Day 7	Baths	1-Breakfast Skillets 2-Quinoa Cup	RESTAURANT	trail mix		
Night 7	Cooper			chips, salsa & guacamole	Pan-Seared Chicken & Lentil Salad	Coconut Chocolate Pudding
Day 8	DEPART	Yogurt Berry Parfait	x	x	x	x

R/highlight=restaurant

X=outside the scope of your trip

*=grocery store with dinghy access

Sample Meal Plans for Specific Diets

To accommodate one or two people in the group who follow a strict and specific diet seems complicated, especially for someone who is not used to eating that way. That is why those individuals with restrictions need to be very involved in the meal planning and provisioning process. Some people recommend that those individuals oversee meal planning and provisioning. I recommend collaboration amongst the group so that everyone's needs are addressed.

The person with the restrictions should be in charge of sourcing and bringing specific substitute items, just in case. Again, spelling out specific needs and restrictions is very important. It is also a good idea to keep certain diet-specific foods separately in the cabin. You don't want a hungry teenager devouring your vegan GF cookies when there are five packs of regular cookies on board.

The good news is that there are many foods that everyone can eat. With some creativity and flexibility, you can create some memorable meals that the whole crew will enjoy. It's impossible to list all the various types of dietary preferences but below are three examples to give you some ideas for lunches and dinners.

The Gluten-Free Vegan

	Lunch	Dinner
Day 1	x	
Night 1	x	R
Day 2	Mixed Bean Salad	
Night 2		R
Day 3	R	
Night 3		Lentil Bolognese with Spaghetti Squash
Day 4	Caribbean Quinoa Salad	
Night 4		Cauliflower Steak with Hummus
Day 5	R	
Night 5		R
Day 6	Lentil Salad	
Night 6		R
Day 7	R	
Night 7		Grilled Tofu with Chimichurri
Day 8	x	x

The Vegetarian/Pescatarian

	Lunch	Dinner
Day 1	x	
Night 1	x	R
Day 2	Cheese Quesadilla	
Night 2		R
Day 3	R	
Night 3		Shrimp and Avocado Salad
Day 4	Ramen Noodle Salad	
Night 4		Seasoned Salmon with Black Bean Salad
Day 5	R	
Night 5		R
Day 6	Egg Salad Sandwich	
Night 6		R
Day 7	R	
Night 7		Artichoke Pasta
Day 8	x	x

The Dairy-Free Meat Lover

	Lunch	Dinner
Day 1	x	
Night 1	x	R
Day 2	Turkey Avocado Pocket	
Night 2		R
Day 3	R	
Night 3		Grilled Steak & Adriatic Potato Salad
Day 4	Deviled Shrimp	
Night 4		Jerk Chicken Fajitas
Day 5	R	
Night 5		R
Day 6	Chicken Waldorf Salad	
Night 6		R
Day 7	R	
Night 7		Herbed Pork Tenderloin & Spicy Corn
Day 8	x	x

CHAPTER 4

PROVISIONING YOUR BOAT

Now that you know a little bit more of what to expect on your upcoming vacation, and you have picked out some specific recipes for food and thought about cocktail hour, which starts very early when you are on a boat, we need to focus on the actual groceries that you will need. This includes where you can buy groceries at the start of your trip, where you can restock, and what you may want to bring from home.

Checking out grocery store websites and looking for specific food items online is easier to do from the comfort of your home. Compile an excel spreadsheet or go simple with a pen and paper. Figuring out quantities of various food items is an important step in the provisioning process, and it requires factoring in the group's ages and activity levels. Most people who don't spend the necessary time calculating quantities either buy too much (and then have hundreds of dollars in leftover food at the end of their charter), or they spend a considerable part of their vacation grocery shopping. Making detailed shopping lists will ultimately save you time and money and increase the likelihood that you won't forget needed items. But first I want to give you some tips regarding a few food groups.

Storing Various Foods Aboard

Before you get excited about eating something specific on your upcoming vacation, learn what is feasible and reasonable to expect aboard a bareboat yacht. Most of the groceries you choose should be shelf-stable and, if they need refrigeration, very compact. Any food that keeps at room temperature in the stores can be kept on the boat at cabin temperature. However, many American specialty items are shipped to the islands in freezers because of the long transport distances. Once those products are thawed, they can spoil quickly. Therefore, they need to be kept frozen on the boat. Similarly, many fruits, such as berries and tomatoes, are refrigerated during shipping and then need to be kept in the refrigerator on the boat. Here are some tips for storing certain food categories on a boat:

Bread and Baked Goods

Locally baked sandwich bread, buns, and muffins are sold on the shelves, just like in U.S. supermarkets, but often become moldy after two to three days at cabin temperature because of the heat and humidity. Fortunately, freshly baked goods are usually available for purchase in smaller markets and bakeries around the islands, so they are easy to restock.

You may not expect to find products such as bagels, English muffins, pita bread, and gluten-free bread in the freezer section at the grocery stores. This is because these products are imported mostly for tourists. Keep them in your boat's freezer until needed. Once defrosted, use them within two days. Tortillas are sold frozen in some stores and kept on the shelves in other stores.

Eggs

Eggs are extremely versatile and are great to have on hand. However, do not purchase more than two dozen eggs at a time because they take up a lot of refrigerator space. They are easy to find at most small grocery stores and bakeries.

Fruit

Fruit is very versatile and comes in various forms—fresh, frozen, canned and dried. It is very refreshing and can be part of many types of meals. Fresh fruit that stores well on the boat at cabin temperature includes:

- Apples, which will keep for one week
- Bananas, which will keep for two to three days (but can be frozen once they start browning)
- Citrus (grapefruit, oranges, clementines, limes and lemons), which will keep for one week
- Grapes, which will keep for two days at cabin temperature (longer if refrigerated)
- Kiwi, which will keep for three to five days
- Mangoes, which will keep for two to five days
- Papaya, which will keep for two to three days
- Pears, which will keep for three to five days
- Pineapple, which will keep for two to three days (lay it on its side, so it does not get moldy on the bottom)
- Plums, which will keep for three to five days
- Soursop, which will keep for two to three days (it is deemed ripe when you can puncture its thick skin with your fingernail)

Frozen fruit is easy to use and requires no prepping or peeling. It will take up freezer space, but it is compact. Mango, berries, pineapple, and smoothie mixes all can be bought frozen. Bananas can be frozen whole. You can defrost them before peeling by letting them sit out in the sun for 5 minutes or by putting them in cold water for a few minutes.

Canned fruit is convenient because it requires no prepping or peeling. However, it will taste better when chilled so put it in your cooler chest for a couple of hours before serving. Pineapples, peaches, pears, mandarin oranges, grapefruit, and mixed fruit cocktail can all be found in cans.

Dried fruits, such as raisins, Craisins, and prunes, are stocked in local stores, but bring dried cherries or apricots from home.

Salads

Green, leafy salads are not practical. They take up too much space in the refrigerator and will often get crushed. I recommend eating green salads in restaurants, unless you have a very small group and a lot of refrigerator space or you will eat the salad greens very soon after you buy them. The salads in this book are more boat-friendly and can either be a main dish or a side dish with grilled fish, chicken, or meat. They utilize canned veggies with an addition of fresh vegetables for crunchiness and flavor.

Vegetables

Vegetables also come in various forms, and you can buy a mix of fresh, frozen, and canned vegetables. However, some of the fresh vegetables you can store at cabin temperature, and others you need to refrigerate just like you see them displayed in grocery stores.

Fresh vegetables that can be stored at cabin temperature include:

- Avocadoes, which will keep for two to three days
- Cabbage, which will keep for two to three days (you can simply discard the outer wilted leaves)
- Onions and fresh garlic, which will keep for up to two weeks
- Potatoes, which will keep for about a week
- Spaghetti squash, which will keep for about a week
- Tomatoes, which will keep for only one to two days

Fresh vegetables that need to be refrigerated but are the most compact and hardiest in terms of bruising include:

- Asparagus
- Carrots
- Celery
- Cucumbers
- Peppers
- Zucchini

I like using frozen vegetables because they are already washed and chopped. If you have freezer space buy broccoli, spinach and mixed vegetable medleys.

As mentioned, many recipes in this book utilize canned vegetables such as:

- Beans (cannellini, white, butter, pink, black, garbanzo, or red kidney)
- Corn
- Diced Tomatoes
- Green beans
- Lentils

Nuts and Seeds

Except for walnuts and pecans, most types of nuts are usually available for purchase. You can also find a variety of mixed nuts.

Ground flaxseed is usually stocked in grocery stores. Chia seeds and hemp seeds are more difficult to find but easy to bring.

Meat and Fish

Because meats need to be stored in the freezer, they need to be boneless and compact. Meat cuts that are best include:

- Chicken breasts
- Chicken tenderloins
- Filet Mignon
- Hamburger patties
- Hot dogs
- New York strip steak
- Pork tenderloin
- Pork chops
- Rib eye steak
- Sausages
- Sirloin steak

Most fish are sold frozen, and fish fillets are best. If you plan on fishing yourself, please familiarize yourself with the warning about reef fish. Some areas have an official warning regarding ciguatera poisoning, a foodborne illness which is caused by a natural toxin found in predatory reef fish in the Caribbean and other tropical islands. Check with local authorities to see if certain types of fish are not recommended to be consumed.

Of course, canned tuna, chicken, and salmon are ideal in terms of storage.

How to Create the Grocery List and Calculate Quantities

Stocking a bareboat charter yacht is a big undertaking, so let's dive into the details. For ease of planning, I recommend making this a two-step process. The first step will be to make a list of groceries for each of the four types of meals listed below and the second step will be to combine those four grocery lists and group them by grocery categories as they are sold in the grocery stores. For example, you may be working on "Beverages," and you plan on making Bloody Mary's, so you will need celery for your cocktails. Put celery on your list so that it will later get added under "Fresh Fruits and Vegetables" (page 51). This example comes to mind because I have given celery stalks to fellow boaters in the marina more than once.

1. Beverages and water
2. Breakfast foods
3. Snacks, appetizers, and desserts
4. Lunches and dinners

You may also want to divide the research process for each type of meal among your group. Look online to find out which brands for certain items the local grocery stores carry, and which of those options your group members prefer. Since storage of food items aboard can be limited, be mindful to only consume the specific food and beverage you asked for and to not consume someone else's favorites.

People tend to eat and drink more on vacation in general but especially when they do water activities and when it is hot. Everyone needs to approximate how much they normally consume at home and then slightly increase those quantities to accommodate the added appetite. Remember, there may not always be a grocery store within easy reach, and you don't want a "hangry" crew, so it's best to buy a little extra.

Don't be surprised by the total number of items on your list and by the total quantities. Provisioning requirements are quite different from what we are used to when grocery shopping at home. Your final grocery list will be long. It will require a lot of calculations, including thinking about portion sizes, and looking at package sizes, and servings per container.

There is a huge disconnect between portion sizes listed on food labels and the portion sizes we are accustomed to seeing when we eat out in restaurants. The usual adult portion size on nutrition labels is ⅓ pound of meat or fish per person. The recipes in this guide allocate ½ pound per person, but if you have young, active adults on board, the portions may need to be more generous. Similarly, most 15-ounce cans of vegetables or beans are enough for two adults. Many salads are suitable either as a main meal or as a side dish. You will need to think about the number of servings accordingly.

In the Appendix you will find a table entitled "Package Sizes and Number of Servings" (page 241), as well as tables with common weights and liquids used in this book. These tables can serve as a quick reference to help you estimate how much to order. This is especially helpful for condiments. For some of the serving sizes I give a range—from what is on the food label to what I find to be realistic.

Sometimes package sizes from different brands will vary slightly. Some foods also weigh more than others even though they are in the same-sized can or jar. Canned goods such as diced tomatoes and beans are a good example. Diced tomato cans list the weight as 14.5 ounces, but canned beans weigh 15.5 ounces, as you will see in various recipes.

While putting together your grocery list, you will deal with a lot of different numbers, so let's illustrate the calculation process with a few examples based on a group of six people on the yacht for a full week. You also need to consider how much time you will be spending in beach bars and going to restaurants when estimating food and beverage consumption.

Water and Beverages

Water for Cooking: We buy water in 1-gallon jugs and always keep one handy near the coffee maker and the sink. When preparing food, you need to adjust to not automatically use water from the tap like you do at home. I use bottled water anytime I make coffee, boil potatoes, cook pasta, or rinse beans from a can. Based on my experience you need about ¼ gallon of water per person per day for cooking. For six people for one week, you will need:

- ¼ x 6 = 1.5 gallons per day = 10.5 gallons total

Water for Drinking: Water can be purchased in gallons or in 16-ounce bottles. For easy reference, one gallon is the equivalent of eight 16-

ounce bottles, and a case of water usually contains 24 bottles. If you have six people, and everyone drinks three bottles or 48 fluid ounces every day, you will need:

- 3 x 6 = 18 bottles per day = ¾ case per day = 5.25 cases for one week.

If your yacht has a 3- to 5-gallon cooler specifically for drinking water aboard, then you can buy drinking water in 1-gallon jugs and refill personal water bottles. For six people the math looks like this:

- 1 gallon = 8 water bottles (16 ounces each)
- 18 bottles per day = 2.25 gallons per day = 15.75 gallons for the week

Beer: In this scenario, four people drink beer with an average of three cans per person per day, and one case of beer is twenty-four cans.

- 3 x 4 = 12 = ½ case per day = 3½ cases of beer for the week

Wine: In this scenario, two people drink white wine, with an average of half a bottle per person per day

- ½ x 2 = 1 bottle per day = 7 bottles of white wine for the week

Coffee: In this scenario, six people drink coffee. Four people drink two cups in the morning only, and two people drink two cups in the morning and one cup in the afternoon.

- (4 x 2) + (2 x 3) = 14 cups per day = 98 cups of coffee for the week

Breakfast Foods

How many people would like eggs in the morning, how many eggs per person, and how many times during your vacation?

Eggs: In this scenario, four people would eat eggs three times during the week. The average is two eggs per person.

- 2 x 4 = 8 eggs per day; 8 eggs x 3 times = 24 eggs for the week = 2 dozen for the week.

Toast / Bread: Quantities are based on two pieces per person per day with six people aboard.

- 2 x 6 = 12 slices of bread / day = ¾ loaf per day = 4½ loaves for the week.

As you can see, quantities are adding up quickly.

Snacks, Appetizers, and Desserts

For any snacks and or packaged foods you plan to buy, you need to find out how many servings are in a bag or a container. Often the serving sizes listed are quite small, so consider how much you really need for one day for your group. Here are two examples:

Fritos: A 9-ounce bag lists nine servings of ten chips per serving. If you double the serving size, you will need two bags for six people.

Hummus: A 10-ounce container lists nine servings of two tablespoons per serving. For six people one container may be enough.

Lunches and Dinners

Once your group has selected the meals for the lunches and dinners, look at the recipes carefully, make any necessary substitutions, and adjust the quantities for your group size. Most of the recipes in this book are written for groups of six. Sandwiches and snacks are for single portions. Salad quantities are given in terms of how many cups they yield. Before making your shopping list, measure out at home what your usual portion of a given salad would be if you had it as a main dish or as a side. That will give you an idea how much you need to adjust the needed quantities. If you make more, the good news is that most of these salads will keep fresh for a day or two. Leftovers always come in handy.

Let's look at the ingredients in the following two recipes from this book (from pages 142 and 218):

Mediterranean Side Salad	
1	cucumber, chopped
1	pint cherry or grape tomatoes, halved
½	red onion, sliced
2	green onions, sliced (optional)
1	3-ounce can black olives, sliced
4	ounces feta cheese crumbles (optional)
3	tablespoons olive oil
2	tablespoons red wine vinegar

Tuna and White Bean Salad	
2	15-ounce cans cannellini beans
4	5-ounce cans albacore tuna
1	cucumber, cubed
½	cup parsley, chopped
½	red onion, thinly sliced
1	3-ounce can black olives
½	red pepper, finely chopped
6	tablespoons lemon juice
6	tablespoons olive oil

Add all the ingredients from the selected recipes to your master grocery list. Combine items that are the same and are used in various recipes. For these two recipes, the grocery list will look like this:

Items for Shopping List	
2	15-ounce cans cannellini beans
4	5-ounce cans albacore tuna
1	pint cherry tomatoes
2	cucumbers
1	red onion
1	lemon
¼	bunch parsley
2	3-ounce cans sliced black olives
½	red bell pepper
4	ounces feta cheese
9	tablespoons olive oil
2	tablespoons red wine vinegar

Once all ingredients are added to the list, the second step will be to group your items into similar grocery categories like you see in the layout of grocery stores: deli, bakery, fresh fruits and vegetables, meat, chilled items (such as packaged deli meats and dips), eggs, cheeses, canned fruit and vegetables, frozen foods (which as we said, can include bagels, tortillas, etc.), condiments, nuts and chips, etc. This will make life easier for both scenarios: ordering online or going to the store in person. For a cheat sheet regarding how groceries are usually grouped in stores and what you can find where, go to **SetSailCookbook.com**.

Take a close look at the chilled foods and the frozen foods. Separate them out to estimate if they will fit into the fridge and freezer space that you will have. I have seen different types of refrigerators on boats. While the style of refrigerators with drawers seems small, a surprising amount of food fits into them because there are no shelves and, thus, no "wasted" space. During our last trip, I tried to "quantify" how much frozen food can fit into the freezer and how much into the refrigerator. I brought with me grocery paper bags from Trader Joe's and from Whole Foods. They are both the same size and are smaller than those from Kroger stores, for example. I was able to accommodate two paper grocery bags of frozen items in the freezer and three grocery bags of chilled items in the refrigerator. So, once you have your grocery list, and if you are worried about the quantities, you can bring those mid-sized paper bags with you to your local grocery store and fill them with the chilled and frozen items from your shopping list to get an idea on quantities.

Once you have your complete list, evaluate what is realistic given your limited space, and adjust your meal plans accordingly. Fresh vegetables take up a lot of space, and the bigger your group, the smaller the quantity of bulky refrigerated foods you should buy. As already mentioned, do not overload on eggs and bread at the start of your trip. Instead, buy what is reasonable for those first few days, and then add eggs and bread to your "Restock List."

Don't Forget General Supplies

Just when you thought you were done, there is one more list. You may need cleaning products, spices, paper goods and personal products such as soap, bug spray, toilet paper, etc. On a bareboat, you usually need to provision everything, but it is a good idea to check with your charter company if they will provide some of these items. Thankfully, all these supplies are easy to store. When ordering, take into account the length of your vacation and that you will use many of these items only partially. On page 56, there are recommendations regarding which of these products you may want to bring from home. Here is a comprehensive list of general items needed based on my experience. Cross out what you don't need, see which items you and your crew will bring with you and put the rest on your grocery list:

- Aluminum foil
- Black pepper
- Cellulose or microfiber cloths (to wipe down tables and seating areas, if wet)
- Clothes pins (for closing chip and cereal bags)
- Dish soap
- Dish sponge/brush/wand
- Lighter fluid
- Matches
- Multipurpose cleaner
- Napkins
- Nonstick spray
- Paper towels
- Paper plates
- Plastic cups
- Propane tank or charcoal
- Reusable grocery bag
- Reusable wine carrier bags (see page 63)
- Salt
- Sandwich bags
- Seasoning mixes
- Toilet paper (1 roll/person/week is usually sufficient)

- Trash bags (13-gallon size)
- Ziplock freezer bags (both quart and gallon size)

Now your provisioning list is complete. I know, you have had to go back and forth on certain items several times to clarify and confirm. "Is this really necessary?" you may be wondering. Well, it is if you want to have the right amount of food. You will, of course, always have some leftover groceries. What I am talking about is a lot of leftover food and drink, because it seemed easier to just order everything from some suggested shopping list instead of thinking about what your group would actually need. I don't like to waste food or money, but in my opinion, an even bigger benefit is that you will be able to relax and enjoy the sun and the sea instead of navigating from one grocery store to another because your group didn't spend time planning and preparing.

Where, How, and When to Provision

You need one point person to check the final shopping list, whether it is the online cart or on paper. Over the years, I have experimented with various planning processes, and one time we had three couples on the boat, each of whom was responsible for several meals. We went to the grocery store, and everyone was supposed to get the ingredients for the meals they were in charge of. Back on the boat, we ended up with twenty avocadoes instead of six. The silver lining is that we found a great recipe online and made "Cold Avocado Soup," which is now part of this book.

When planning your grocery and food supply pickups, ask your charter company or agent which stores they recommend. Go online to see what grocery items the stores carry and how user-friendly their websites are. You will need to find many different items, so ease of navigating the websites matters. Once you know what the stores carry, you may have follow-up questions for your group; for example, if stores don't offer your preferred item, is it okay to get a different brand or flavor?

After you learn what the main grocery stores are, find out if specialty stores exist. For example, in the British Virgin Islands you have:

General Grocery Stores:
- Bobby's Marketplace: www.bobbyssupermarket.com
- Rite Way Food Markets: www.rtwbvi.com

Specialty Stores:
- Wine and Spirits: TICO at www.ticobvi.com or Caribbean Cellars at www.caribbeancellars.com
- Locally Grown Fruits and Vegetables: Good Moon Farm at www.MoonFarms.com
- European Imports: The French Deli at www.frenchdelibvi.com
- Specialty Food Items: Relish Gourmet Wines & Beverages at www.relishgourmetfoods.com
- Meat and Seafood: Steakation at www.bvibutcher.com

There will be a lot of food. I highly recommend spending the time at home and before arrival to place your provisioning order online and have it delivered directly to the boat. This works well most of the time and is by far the most convenient and efficient way to do it. The likelihood of the main store having most of the items that you need is greater when you order ahead of time than when you go in person. Placing food orders online also gives you the option of ordering items from various specialty stores and having them delivered. The delivery fees are reasonable and worth it. At the very least, order water, drinks, and shelf-stable items to be delivered. Those items are bulky and heavy but don't need refrigeration, so there is usually more flexibility with delivery times.

If delivery is not an option and you have to go in person, your grouped items on your shopping list will be helpful and save you time in the store, especially if you assign a couple of categories to members of your group. After all, you want to get back to your yacht as quickly as possible so you can head out onto the beautiful waters.

Things to consider as you think about the logistics of grocery shopping:
- How much are the delivery fees?
- How much are taxis?
- How many people need to go to the grocery store?

- What time are you arriving? Will stores be open at that time? Is delivery available after that time?
- How much time will grocery shopping take? Two, three, or four hours?

Ask the charter company for any grocery store and online ordering recommendations. Individual stores provide information on their websites about order lead times. Usually, it is a good idea to order food one week ahead of your scheduled arrival to be delivered around the time you expect to arrive on your charter yacht.

Find out what your yacht's name will be. When you place your online order, you will usually specify the name of the charter company, the name of the yacht, and a time window for delivery. We usually get orders delivered to the boat from several stores. Ask your charter company and the grocery store you order from about what to do in case your arrival is delayed for any reason. You do not want your food to sit on the dock in front of your boat for several hours. Most of the time someone either from the charter company or the food delivery person will put your frozen items into the freezer and the chilled items into the fridge. Make sure you arrange to tip that person if possible.

If ordering online, check the box to allow for substitutions. There are times when certain items are nowhere to be found—at least, not until the next cargo ship arrives. When a substitution box is selected, the store can replace your requested item with a similar brand. A substitution is better than nothing. This is how provisioning and grocery shopping works on islands, and it is part of the adventure.

If you order online, the receipt will usually list all the items that they were not able to fulfill. Often, they will email you that receipt the night before delivery. Before heading out of the marina, check if you can find those items nearby or add them to your "Restock List."

Also, find out from your charter company where dinghy-accessible stores are located and what products they carry (i.e. eggs, bread, fruit). Most of them will carry water, beer, and snack foods. So, no worries— you will have those. Based on your itinerary, estimate when you might be in that location. Order enough perishable items initially to last you until you reach that location to restock. Put grocery restocking into your itinerary (page 27) or play it by ear but have the list of stores handy.

For example, in the British Virgin Islands these stores are all easily accessible by dinghy and a short walk from the dinghy dock:

- Bobby's Supermarket in Cane Garden Bay
- Christine's Bakery at Jost Van Dyke
- Harbor Market at West End/Soper's Hole
- JVD Grocery at Jost Van Dyke
- Rite Way at Nanny Cay
- Rudy's at Jost Van Dyke
- Scrub Island Marina
- The Chef's Pantry at Leverick Bay
- Trellis Bay Superette

Be aware that transferring grocery bags from the dock to the dinghy and then to the boat can be challenging if there is wind or there are waves. One time we had an emergency. Someone called out "EGGS OVERBOARD!" just after we returned to the boat. I turned around and saw two egg cartons and other groceries floating around the boat. We jumped in and retrieved our food—well, most of it. The people on the boat next to us got a good laugh. Remarkably, the eggs were just fine.

What to Bring from Home

Here are some suggestions and recommendations of what to bring with you for your vacation. As you will see, I will mention some non-food items as well, but everything has a connection to food or eating, whether aboard or ashore.

Money: More specifically, you need to bring cash. In the British Virgin Islands, the U.S. dollar is the official currency. Check what the local currency is in your destination, and find out how much cash you will need for a typical charter yacht vacation for a certain number of days. For example, in the BVI daily expenses for ice, trash disposal, and mooring fees will run from $60 to $100 per day, depending on how many chest coolers you have and how quickly your ice melts. For a one-week vacation, I would recommend that each person bring at least $200 in cash with them, since you will also need cash for entry and exit fees at customs and for cab rides to your base or to the grocery stores. Tips for boat briefings, repair services, and fuel dock attendants are also customary.

Multiple Credit Cards: To pay for your groceries, you can usually use a credit card. Be aware that American Express cards are not accepted by some grocery stores, so make sure you have other types of credit cards with you, as well. We had that experience in the Bahamas as well as in the BVI.

Flashlight: When going out to eat at restaurants in the evening, keep in mind that the closer you are to the equator the sooner it gets dark at night. In the Caribbean it is often dark by 7:30 p.m. Therefore, it is a good idea to bring a flashlight for dinghy rides back to your boat after dinner. Also consider using a little ribbon or bandana to mark your dinghy—they all look alike next to each other on the dinghy dock, and it is easy to jump into the wrong one.

Spices and Seasonings: For a seven-day trip, one bottle of each should be more than enough—or even just a few teaspoons in a small sandwich bag. If the spice contains garlic or cumin, however, make sure to pack it in an outside pocket of your luggage, or bring it in a bottle. You don't want your clothes to smell. Here are the spices that are used in this book and that work well for preparing fish, chicken, and red meat:

- Black pepper mill (small)
- Caribbean jerk seasoning
- Crushed red pepper flakes
- Ground cinnamon
- Herbs de Provence
- Italian seasoning
- Seafood seasoning
- Steak seasoning

Food Items: You should bring any hard-to-find ingredients or specific flavors of a certain item to the boat. Having what you need will give you peace of mind and help you relax. Most dehydrated and powdered foods are easy to pack.

- Bacon bits
- Bouillon cubes

- Chocolate bars
- Cocoa powder
- Coconut flakes
- Dried cherries / apricots
- Instant mashed potatoes
- Lemonade powders
- 90-second rice pouches
- Oatmeal packets
- Protein bars
- Protein powders
- Pure vanilla extract
- Ranch dip packets
- Seeds (chia, flax, etc.)
- Sugar
- Sweet'N Low / Stevia (sweetener packets or drops)
- Teabags
- Walnuts / pecans

Nonfood Items for the Galley:

I highly recommend bringing the first four items listed below. Consider the others only if you plan on cooking a fair amount.

- Dish wand with a detergent dispenser handle—it saves water and manicures
- Resealable freezer bags (quart- and gallon-size)
- Cellulose cloths or reusable kitchen towels for wiping down wet seating areas, tables, and kitchen counters
- Clothes pins for closing snack bags as well as hanging clothes to dry (six to eight per person)
- Two to four plastic storage containers with lids (6- to 8-cup size, rectangular)
- Sandwich bags, a few always come in handy
- One to two thin cutting boards, so everyone can participate in meal preparation
- Small measuring cup for making cocktails
- Meat thermometer for grilling and pan-frying

- Microwave egg cooker
- Multipurpose or food gloves for handling fresh garlic or raw jalapeños

As you can see, there are many things to think about when planning a charter yacht vacation. The lists and suggestions I have provided so far will be useful for starting your group's planning process, as you embark on a completely new adventure. I have summarized the timeline for preparations in the Preparation Timeline table below starting with setting realistic expectations and up to arrival day.

<h3 style="text-align:center">Preparation Timeline</h3>

When	What to do
Ten weeks before	• Set realistic expectations and start thinking about your vacation
Eight weeks before	• Gather input from charter company and group
Six weeks before	• Plan your itinerary and pick restaurants where you would like to eat
Five weeks before	• Pick out recipes and make a meal plan
Four weeks before	• Try out some of the chosen recipes • Focus on quantities and serving sizes
Three weeks before	• Finalize meal plan
Two weeks before	• Make your five shopping lists • If ordering online, create account for group, so input of groceries can be a shared effort • The point person for food needs to double check quantities to avoid duplication • If you will be shopping in person, group your items on the grocery list to correspond with how grocery stores are generally laid out • Estimate how many chilled and frozen items you have in your cart or on your list

One to two weeks before	• Input online orders for beverages, groceries, and specialty foods • Let your charter company know which deliveries they need to expect • The sooner you place your order, the more likely it is that you will get your desired time slot for delivery • Shop at home for items you can't order locally or that you want/need – everyone can bring a few items
Arrival Day	• Go grocery shopping if you have to do it in person—think about logistics such as taxis, carts, etc.—you will have lots of food; ask your charter company for recommendations • Go grocery shopping to supplement any missing or forgotten items if you have a small store in the marina • Start your "Restock List"

We hope your travels will go smoothly and that everything will go as planned. The very last part of the preparation process will take place once everyone arrives on the charter yacht and before you set sail. Arrival day is a busy and exciting day. More on that in the next chapter.

CHAPTER 5

BEFORE YOU LEAVE THE MARINA

Once you arrive on your yacht, you will have so much fun exploring the boat. As you unpack, you find all kinds of cubbies and storage compartments in your cabin where you can stow your personal items. Hopefully your provisions have been delivered, and you already have a refreshing drink in one hand. With clear blue skies above, you can't wait to set sail. But before you leave the marina, be sure to complete the following tasks to set yourself up for a successful and stress-free sailing adventure.

Put Away Provisions

Put away all the food securely, as anything that can fly will fly once you hit waves. Take special precautions with wine and liquor bottles, as you do not want broken glass anywhere on the boat. Speaking of wine bottles, the first night we ever spent on a yacht we could not sleep. It was not only because of excitement but also because there was this unusual noise as we tried to fall asleep. Turning on the generator and air conditioners had created a certain hum and vibration on the boat. The gentle, but constant movement of the yacht had caused the wine bottles to come in contact with each other, making a very unusual rattling noise. For a long time, we couldn't even figure out where the noise was coming from. Now, we bring reusable wine carrier bags from home to store all glass bottles in, and we let the gentle waves rock us to sleep.

While you organize and secure all the food, you may notice that some food items are missing. Put those items on the "Restock List." If by any chance someone else has already put your food away, check the refrigerator and freezer to make sure all the items are indeed in the correct spot. You also need to allow for some airflow in the freezer; otherwise, it will not work uniformly. Put as many beverages as possible in the chest coolers to make more space in your fridge.

Before heading out to your first destination, remove and toss all trash, especially cardboard boxes, where bugs can hide. Check your pasta boxes, and anything else that contains flour, for bugs. Can you tell that we've had some experience with this?

Boat Briefing and Inventory

Usually someone from the charter company comes aboard to give you a boat briefing before you head out. They explain how to use all the navigation instruments, how to turn on the generator and air conditioners, what all the switches on the electrical panel do, etc. They go through a lot of information, and your captain will usually focus more on the mechanical and technical aspects. However, details surrounding the galley are important as well.

Go to the kitchen and test all the appliances. Become familiar with the generator and which appliances require the use of the generator. As your galley appliances will be new to you, be sure that several members of your crew become familiar with them before leaving the marina. Ask specific questions during your orientation such as how to regulate the refrigerator and freezer temperatures. Where is the coldest area within the refrigerator? How to turn on your cooktop or stove? If you plan on grilling, learn how to operate the grill. Test to see if it works. Do you have charcoal, propane, lighter fluid, matches, etc.? Do you need aluminum foil or an aluminum pan for easier clean-up? Similarly, turn on the coffee maker, and toaster to make sure they work. If you have a blender, put some water in it and run it to make sure it doesn't leak. Many yachts have quick turnaround times between charters and sometimes little things get overlooked.

The boat briefing is a very opportune time to identify and call out any missing items in your galley. To prepare and serve meals using the recipes in this book, you need to have a certain set of essential dishes on hand. Take an inventory of your pots and pans so you know what condition they are in. If you have an induction cooktop, are the pots and pans compatible? Try them out. Are the frying pans large enough for your group and not scratched? The knives are often dull, so check them.

You will probably not have platters and fancy serving dishes, but do you have enough plates, glasses and silverware for everyone? Is there a can opener on board? The second time we chartered a yacht, there were eight of us, and we planned to have most of our meals aboard. As you know by now, that meant maximizing canned foods. During our first charter the previous year we had a can opener on board, so we just assumed that one would be aboard again. Typically, that is the case. But it turned out that there was no can opener anywhere in the galley, and it took us four days to find one to buy. That is how we learned where all the dinghy-accessible stores are in the BVI.

For your convenience, I have included two checklists in the appendix and on my website **SetSailCookbook.com**—one with the questions you need to ask during your boat briefing and another with a list of essential dishes and utensils. Your charter company will probably give you an inventory list that includes many other items. Go through that list as well. Sometimes, completely unexpected items are missing. For example, last year, on our third day of vacation our dinghy's outboard motor died while we were returning to our yacht from the beach. It was only then that we realized, as the current was taking us away, that the dinghy paddles were missing, but that is a story for another time.

Galley Tips

When vacationing out in the open water surrounded by salty sea air, how your food keeps and cooks is a little different than cooking on land. For example, one thing I have not been able to master over the past decade is how to cook rice on the boat. I can do it at home just fine but not in the Caribbean's warm and humid climate with the pots that are provided by the charter companies. Having tried many brands and varieties, I have given up on all except for the precooked rice pouches that take 90 seconds to reheat in the microwave. Here are some tips and tricks I have discovered over time on how to keep your food fresh and your recipes delicious. These are not exhaustive lists, just some helpful suggestions:

General:

- Check the refrigerator setting daily—sometimes food accidentally touches the dial and turns it to a higher temperature. Anytime something seems out of the ordinary in the refrigerator or freezer, check the temperature dial.
- Don't put vegetables in the coldest section of the refrigerator—they may freeze.
- For frequently used items, such as coffee cream or mayo, designate a certain spot for them so that everyone knows where to find them and where to return them. For example, creamer is in the front left corner and mayo is in the front right corner. This will minimize how long your refrigerator will stay open each time someone needs to grab something.
- Make sure everyone shuts the refrigerator and freezer doors completely.
- Turn off the grill after each use.
- Know when you need to turn on the generator, so you don't deplete your house batteries.
- If you are making a pasta dish and cannot accommodate a large pot and a large sauté pan on your stove at the same time, start boiling the pasta and, after half of the recommended cooking time, remove it from the burner, and cover it. The pasta will continue cooking, so check its doneness at the recommended time and drain it. Meanwhile, make your sauce and combine everything at the end.

Produce:

- When cooking or meal planning, first use up bulky foods from the refrigerator or those foods that will spoil quickly.
- Don't confuse "cooking bananas" with regular bananas—they look very similar to regular bananas, but they taste very different. They are smaller and greener, and most stores carry them since they are a common food staple in the Caribbean. They taste more like a potato or root vegetable when you boil them, not at all sweet. If unsure, ask at checkout.
- Once the bananas are overripe, put them in the freezer; you can freeze them whole and use them for smoothies. Putting them in warm water for a minute will defrost them enough so you can peel them.
- If given the option, buy red or Yukon gold potatoes; they don't need to be peeled and will save you a step in the preparation process.
- Avocados are ripe when they are firm but with a gentle give when pressed. Once they are ripe, store them in the refrigerator to prevent them from becoming mushy.
- Put prepared salads into gallon-size freezer bags if space is tight in the refrigerator.
- Chop parsley or cilantro and put it in a jar with oil. It will save space, keep fresh, and you can add it to dressings and foods quickly.
- If you like to cook with lots of garlic, buy it in jars already chopped or use garlic salt.
- If you plan on making several pasta meals, but you have one person who is gluten-free, cooking a whole spaghetti squash may be the answer. Cooked spaghetti squash noodles can be made ahead and refrigerated for three to four days and reheated in the microwave. See instructions on page 217.
- If you don't have a lemon/lime juicer, cut the lemon/lime in half crosswise and twist a fork in each half to release the juice.

Proteins:

- Don't cook shrimp in the microwave. It will become rubbery, chewy and dry.
- Many recipes in this book utilize fully cooked large frozen shrimp because it is readily available. If for any reason you end up with raw frozen shrimp, no worries. It is easy to cook. First, let it thaw by adding water directly into the shrimp bag for about fifteen to thirty minutes. Bring 2 to 3 quarts of water to boil in a large pot. Add the shrimp, and cook for two to three minutes or until it turns pink. Drain it, and put shrimp in cold water to stop the cooking process. This will ensure it stays nice and tender. Drain it again and pat dry with paper towels before adding to any recipe.
- To thaw individually packaged fish filets, place them in a bowl or the kitchen sink filled with cold water. Leave them immersed for about fifteen to twenty minutes. Remove filets from the packaging as soon as the fish is thawed. Then season or marinate fish to taste.
- Marinate meat, tofu and fish in gallon-size zip-lock freezer bags.
- Grill extra chicken breasts while making dinner and have those ready to put on top of a salad the next day for lunch.
- See if you can buy already cooked or grilled chicken meat.
- Pan-seared or grilled tofu can be stored in the refrigerator for several days and added to various dishes.
- Cook quinoa in vanilla almond milk or coconut milk if you want it to be sweet and creamy. Cooked quinoa can be kept in the refrigerator for several days. See cooking instructions on page 215.

Nonfood Items/Other:

- To defrost or warm up English muffins, bagels, tortillas or pita bread, just put the whole bag in full sun for twenty to thirty minutes, turning it once.

- Use nonstick cooking spray in addition to oil/butter on the skillets to make clean-up easier. You can also use non-stick spray on grill grates before you start preheating the grill.
- If you have an electric grill, you can use it to make a larger quantity of toast quickly.
- Always cover the pot with a lid when trying to bring water to a boil.
- Add white vinegar to dish soap. It will cut grease, especially if your water is not hot.
- White vinegar is also a remedy for many jellyfish stings, except for Portuguese man-of-war. According to the book *Marine Medicine*, one should, "keep a bottle of vinegar nearby when swimming or diving in waters with jellyfish." Luckily, we have never had to use it.
- Use paper plates if you plan to cook a lot to reduce the number of dishes to be washed by hand.

Now you are truly ready for your vacation. You have everything you need; you have safely stowed all breakable items and groceries; you have become familiar with the yacht's galley; and you know where all the drinks and snacks are. You are ready for some charter yacht fun.

NEVENA MRDALJ

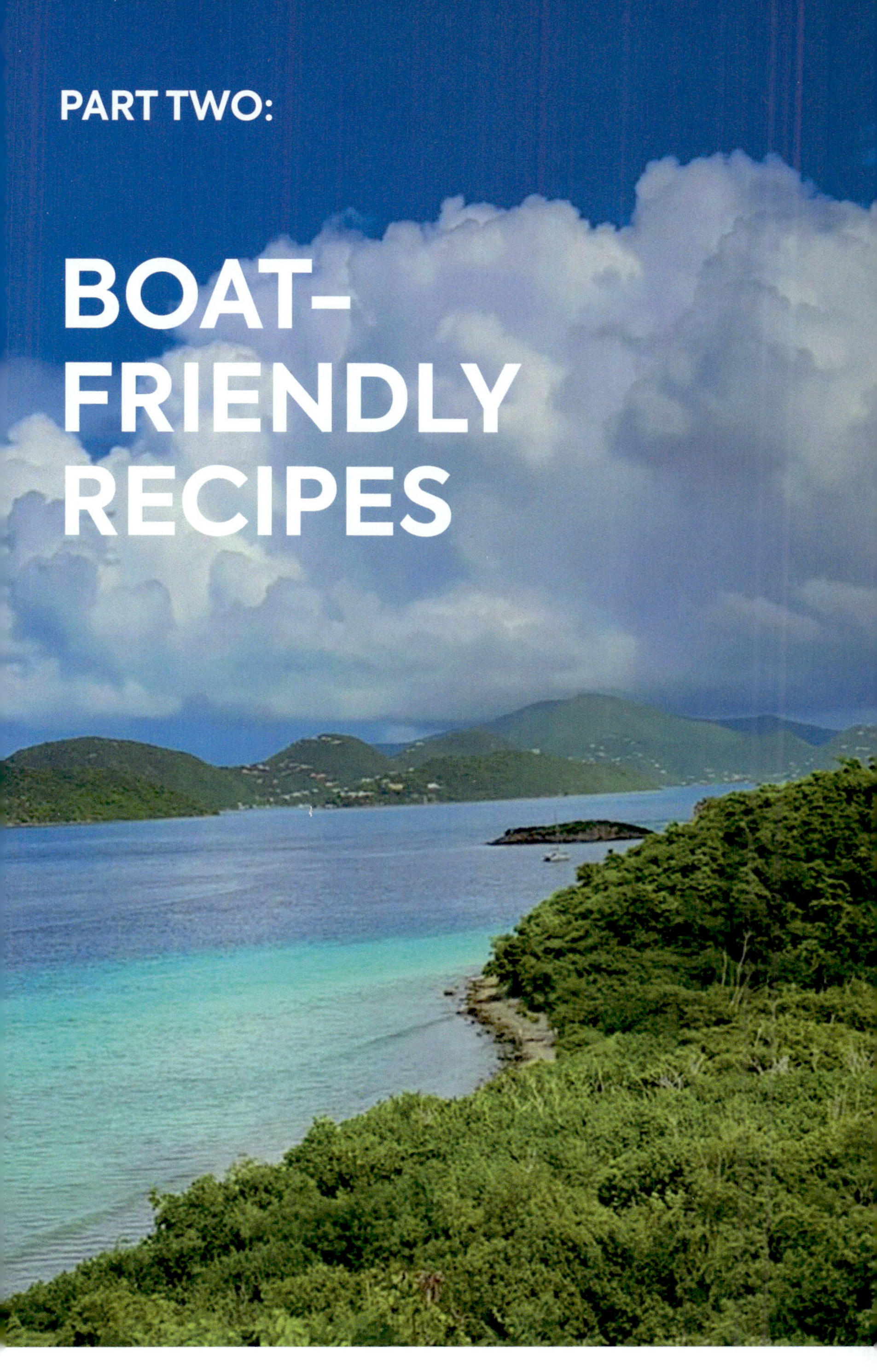

PART TWO:

BOAT–
FRIENDLY
RECIPES

Most of the food and drink that you regularly consume at home you also will be able to enjoy on your charter yacht vacation. Sometimes I marvel at what we can prepare in the middle of the ocean. Everything seems to taste better. That is either because everyone has more of an appetite or because of the ambiance. You don't need to prepare a gourmet meal, just a good meal that hits the spot in the warm climate.

Over the past decade, I have tested and tried out many different recipes and suggestions. This book contains boat-friendly recipes best suited for a tropical climate. Most of the dishes are a fusion of classic Italian, French, Greek, and American meals alongside some Caribbean spices. There are recipes for all types of dietary needs, from the dairy-free meat lover to the gluten-free vegan. You can grill tofu for one person and steak for the others at the same time. Hopefully, when looking at these menu options, everyone in your group will be able to pick out a few items and say, "That sounds good! I could eat that."

Preparing food on a yacht is not only a memorable experience but also very cost-effective. In 2024 in the BVI, excluding alcoholic beverages, the groceries for the recipes outlined in this section were a little less than $200 per person for seven days and included seven breakfasts, eight lunches/dinners, snacks, soft drinks, and water. You may get sticker shock when you first see your grocery receipts, but remember to divide the total amount by the number in your group, and you will feel much better.

In my recipe directions, I try to minimize the number of dishes dirtied, and therefore I present a lot of shortcuts. After all, you are there to have fun, not to be in the galley all day.

Twelve Reasons Why the Recipes in this Book are Boat-Friendly

1. They take thirty minutes or less to prepare as a group.
2. They are easy, delicious, foolproof, and mostly healthy.
3. They are flexible, allowing for omissions, additions, and substitutions.
4. They are suitable for many different dietary needs and are labeled accordingly.
5. They maximize the use of shelf-stable items.

6. They use fruits and vegetables that can be stored at cabin temperature.

7. They have a mix of chilled and frozen items so that the refrigerator and freezer space are fully utilized.

8. They use few pans and dishes for preparation, which makes clean-up easy.

9. The ingredients are consistently available and easy to find. They are the same ones that most U.S. grocery stores carry.

10. The recipes are detailed so you don't forget to order all the necessary condiments and ingredients in the correct quantities when you assemble the grocery list.

11. They utilize simple ingredients in various combinations.

12. They have easy-to-follow directions.

The selection of recipes in this guide tries to accommodate a wide spectrum of dietary needs and, therefore, I have included dietary labels with almost every recipe. Please analyze each recipe individually to see if it fits your dietary restrictions. For quick reference, you can find the definitions in the "Dietary Labels" table (below or page 74). These definitions are limited to the ingredients mentioned in this book and are not comprehensive. If you and your group want to be able to see the recipes grouped by specific labels such as gluten-free, vegan, etc., please visit **SetSailCookbook.com**.

Dietary Labels

V	Vegan	Contains no animal products
V-a	V-adaptable	Ingredients may be omitted or substituted to make dish vegan
VGT	Vegetarian	Contains no meat or fish but may contain milk, cheese or eggs.
VGT-a	VGT-adaptable	Ingredients may be omitted or substituted to make dish vegetarian
DF	Dairy-free	Contains no animal milk or cheese products
DF-a	DF-adaptable	Ingredients may be omitted or substituted to make dish dairy-free
GF	Gluten-free	Contains no grains that contain gluten
GF-a	GF-adaptable	Ingredients may be omitted or substituted to make dish gluten-free
SF	Shellfish	Contains shrimp or lobster
M	Red meat	Contains beef, pork, or lamb
P	Poultry	Contains chicken or turkey
F	Fish	Contains fish
NA	Nonalcoholic	Does not contain alcohol

CHAPTER 6

BEVERAGES

A vacation in a hot climate will lead to the need for a variety of drinks to quench that thirst—from water and cocktails to soft drinks and more. Groceries are a little more expensive on the islands due to added transportation costs, and the money wasted in leftover beverages can add up to a lot. For example, soft drinks cost about $1 per can. You can avoid buying way too much by methodically going through the list below and asking each member of your group to estimate how many bottles/cans/ounces of their favorite beverages they consume daily. Then multiply that by the total number of days of your charter. Keep in mind the setting and that in warm weather everyone might drink more than usual. If by any chance you run out, buying more beverages is easy. Water, beer, wine, spirits and soft drinks are stocked in almost all the island stores.

Here is a list of beverages to help you start the conversation.

Water

Obviously, water is a must and in Chapter 4 (page 47) I have laid out the calculation process for estimating how much water you will need for general cooking. Individual water consumption varies a lot, especially knowing that you will be consuming many other alcoholic and nonalcoholic beverages as well. Still, everyone should try to estimate how much water they will need to stay hydrated. You may also want to use bottled water for brushing teeth.

Coffee and Tea

For many, coffee—whether its regular or decaf, hot or iced—is a must in the morning. Drip coffee makers are usually provided on boats. Your group will need to agree on which brand everyone will drink since you will be making pots of coffee. Maxwell House, Folgers, and other big brands are available locally, or you can bring your favorite brand of coffee from home. Just make sure the coffee is ground! Typically, a 12- to 16-ounce bag of ground coffee will make about sixty cups. How many cups of coffee will your group drink daily? For iced coffee, make a more potent brew, and pour it over ice cubes in a tall glass.

Don't forget that you will also need two to six coffee filters per day (morning and afternoon brews). Ask the charter company which coffee machine it will supply and what type of filters it uses in case you need to supply your own.

Other things to think about that go with coffee:

- Sugar
- Zero-calorie sweetener
- Dairy milk/creamer
- Nondairy milk/creamer
- Powdered creamer

Many types of tea are available at grocery stores, but if you like a specific brand, bring it with you. Check if a pitcher is provided in case someone wants to have iced tea.

Milk and Juice

Local grocery stores usually carry milk and juices in Tetra Paks or carton packaging. The product and the package are sterilized separately and then combined and sealed in a sterile environment. This process enables long shelf lives without refrigeration for the products until they are opened. Milk cartons often will be labeled as UHT (ultra-high temperature), meaning that the milk was ultra-pasteurized.

Nowadays, even on the islands, there are many options for milk such as regular, two percent, skim, soy, oat, coconut, or almond milk. Milk products come in various types of packaging. When ordering, pay attention to whether it needs to be refrigerated before opening and how much space it will take up in the refrigerator.

Many tropical fruit juices are also available in shelf-stable cartons. Juice in general can be kept in chest coolers.

Soft Drinks and Mixers

Most of the popular soft drinks such as Coke and Sprite products are stocked locally. Flavored sparkling waters and energy drinks are available as well. You can buy traditional mixers such as tonic and club soda and also try Caribbean favorites such as Ting, which is a grapefruit soda made in Jamaica. Do you already know what drinks your group is planning to make? Of course, margarita or Bloody Mary mixes make it a breeze to make a cocktail quickly.

Beer and Wine

For some, it may not feel like a true vacation unless they can unwind with a cocktail, beer, or a glass of wine. Light, crisp lagers such as Carib, Presidente, or Red Stripe are easy to drink and perfect for enjoying with lunch or while relaxing. If you plan on ordering beer, cans are preferred. They are lighter, and they can be crushed for disposal, reducing the amount of trash that you will have. Also, with cans, there's zero chance of broken glass on board.

Choosing the right wines will also require group input. Will you need to buy wine that goes with steak or to pair with shrimp? Do you have group members who want a particular Chardonnay no matter what is served, or will you be indulging in Champagne? Are mimosas on your list of requests from your group? Who drinks rosé? These are fun conversations to have and certainly make for fun potlucks as well. Since wine is expensive, spending some time doing the math around planned consumption will be well worth it.

Cocktails

Yachts, sea breezes, and cocktails go hand in hand. You may already have several cocktails in mind and know exactly which ingredients you need for them. There are constantly new products coming on the market so check with your group for their ideas. It's always nice to try something new. In the Caribbean, rum is made locally and exported worldwide, so try some. Of course, all other types of spirits are available also. Don't forget mixers and garnishes for your cocktails such as lemons, limes, oranges, olives, salt, bitters, and celery. Consider bringing a small measuring glass to get the proportions just right.

Trying out local cocktails at beach bars and restaurants is fun. Here are a few recipes in case you want to make them yourself. There are also some refreshing nonalcoholic options, which are perfect not only for the dinghy captain, but are great for little sailors too.

THE JVD COCKTAIL

A classic originating from the Jost Van Dyke Island.

Makes 1 Serving

 **INGREDIENTS**

 **PREPARATION**

2	ounces dark rum
4	ounces pineapple juice
1	ounce mango juice
1	ounce coconut water
½	ounce Campari

1. Mix together all ingredients.
2. Serve "on the rocks."

NEVENA MRDALJ

THE BVI PAINKILLER

Visit each island and find out who makes the best one.

Makes 1 Serving

 **INGREDIENTS**

 **PREPARATION**

3	ounces dark rum
4	ounces pineapple juice
1	ounce orange juice
1	ounce cream of coconut
	Sprinkle of nutmeg

1. Combine all liquid ingredients.
2. Serve "on the rocks" and garnish with fresh ground nutmeg.

RUM PASSION

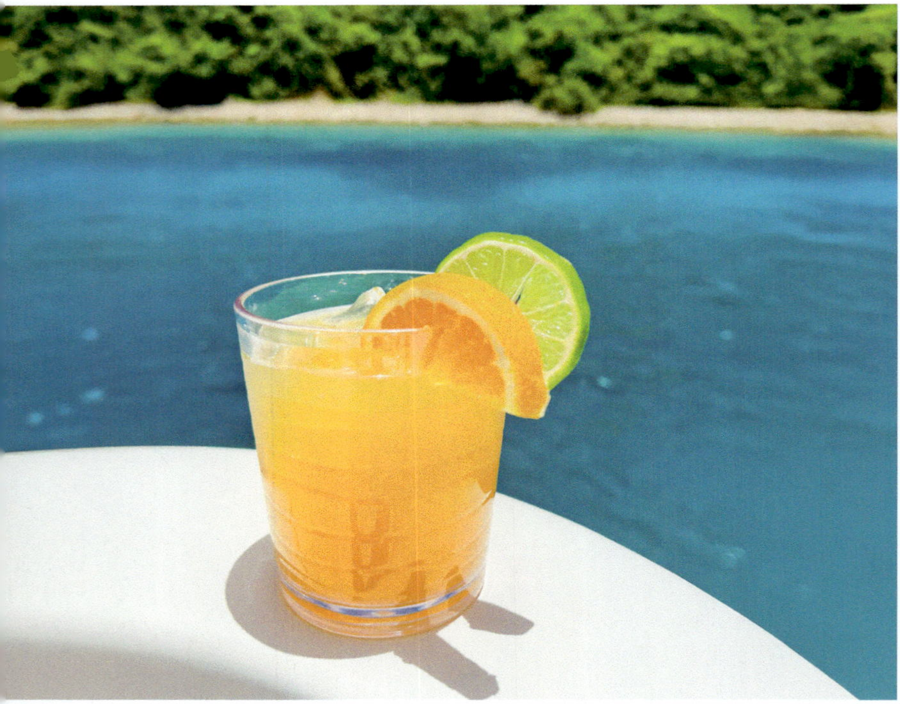

Makes 6 Servings

 **INGREDIENTS**

 **PREPARATION**

1½	cups white rum
1½	cups passion fruit juice
1½	cups pineapple juice
1½	cups mango juice
½	ounce dark rum float for each glass

1. Combine white rum and juices in a pitcher and stir well.

2. Serve "on the rocks" and top off each glass with dark rum.

TING WITH A STING

The Jamaican grapefruit soda makes this drink quite refreshing.

Makes 1 Serving

 **INGREDIENTS**

 **PREPARATION**

2	ounces liquor: rum, citrus vodka, or Campari
5	ounces Ting

1. Mix together all ingredients.
2. Serve "on the rocks."

TROPICAL SEABREEZE (NA)

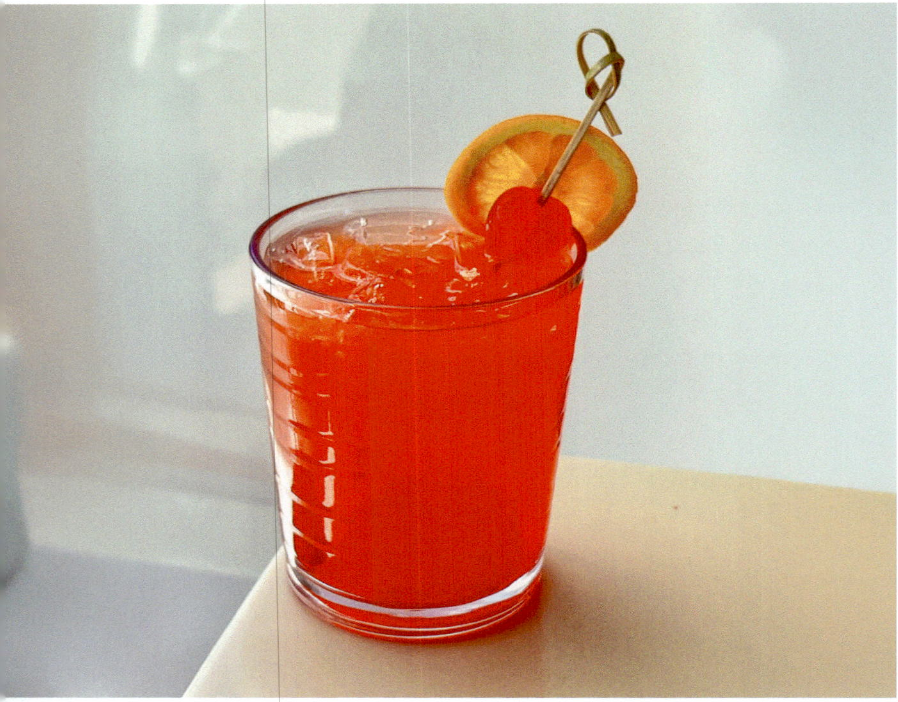

Makes 1 Serving

 **INGREDIENTS**

 **PREPARATION**

4 ounces passion fruit juice	1. Combine all the liquid ingredients.
2 ounces coconut water	2. Serve "on the rocks" and garnish
1 ounce grenadine	with a twist of lemon.
½ ounce lemon juice, freshly squeezed	
Twist of lemon	

GUAVA SPRITZER (NA)

A reminder for your palate that you are in a tropical setting.

Makes 1 Serving

 **INGREDIENTS**

 **PREPARATION**

⅔ cup guava juice

⅓ cup sparkling water or club soda

Lime wedge

1. Combine the liquid ingredients.

2. Serve "on the rocks" and garnish with a lime wedge.

PASSION FANTASY (NA)

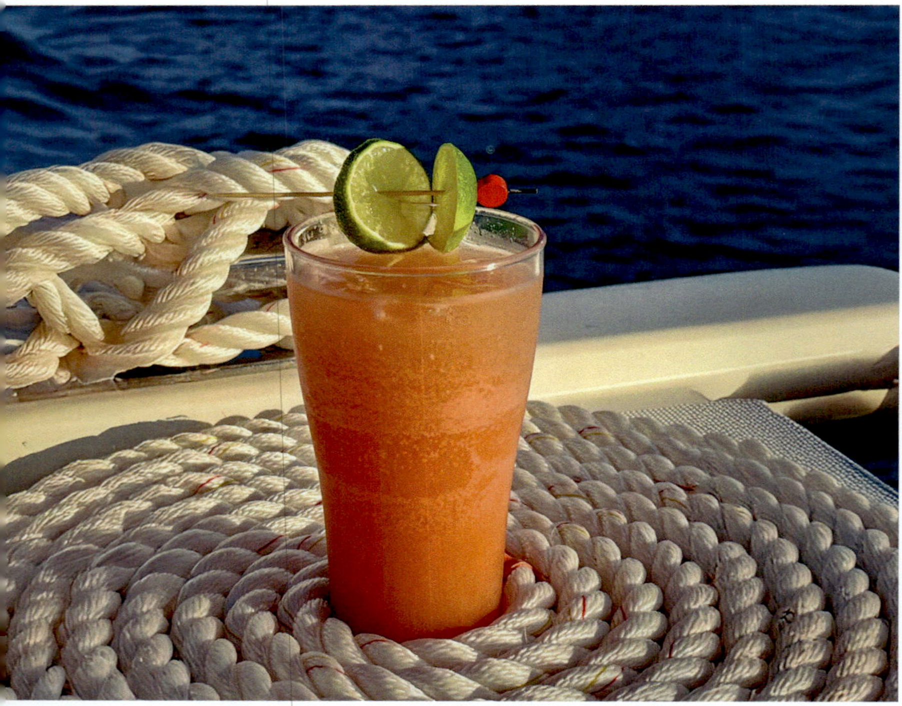

Makes 1 Serving

 **INGREDIENTS**

 **PREPARATION**

3	ounces pineapple juice
2	ounces passion fruit juice
1	tablespoon lemon juice
1	tablespoon grenadine
1	lemon wedge

1. Combine all liquid ingredients.
2. Serve "on the rocks" and garnish with citrus fruit.

THE DRY TONIC (NA)

Great for sipping throughout the day while sailing.

Makes 1 Serving

 **INGREDIENTS**

 **PREPARATION**

6   ounces tonic water

Dash of Angostura aromatic bitters

Squeeze of lime juice

1. Combine all ingredients.
2. Serve "on the rocks."

CHAPTER 7

BREAKFAST FOODS

Breakfast is the most consumed meal on the boat. Everyone has their own morning routine and can make their own breakfast when they feel like it. I may grab something that I have had hundreds of times before, but now, sitting on the bow of the boat looking through the crystal clear water at the rocks on the ocean floor and feeling the gentle lapping of waves against the hull, eating a very ordinary breakfast becomes a memorable experience.

Quick Options

Cereal with milk, protein bars, yogurt and granola, oatmeal packets, rice cakes, bagels with cream cheese, and peanut butter with fruit are all good breakfast options on a boat. They are quick and easy to prepare. They can be eaten at any time. If someone needs to have a specific brand, many of the dry foods can be easily brought from home. As mentioned, many types of milk—such as almond, oat and coconut—are now stocked in stores that provision boat charters.

Everyone seems to like cold smoothies on a boat, even if they normally do not have smoothies at home. You can add protein powders and various seeds to make them very filling. Several recipes utilizing local fruits are provided in this section.

Having banana bread, coconut bread, empanadas, muffins, brownies and cookies as well as freshly baked bread for breakfast is always a treat. I like trying locally made pastries and supporting the hardworking people of the islands. These items are available at local bakeries and grocery stores. Sometimes you can also buy them at stands near dinghy docks or from boats that sell ice.

Eggs are versatile and a great type of food on a boat. You can cook them sunny side up, scramble them, or boil them. You can accommodate portion sizes individually by cooking the desired number of eggs for each person.

Hardboiled eggs are very convenient to have on hand to use for a quick snack, to make egg salad or to put on avocado toast. They are also easy to cook on a boat. Add eggs to boiling water and boil for about 4 minutes. Remove the pan from heat, cover it, and let it sit for 10 more minutes. Then put the eggs in cold water, and, once they have completely cooled, store them in the refrigerator for up to one week. Label them so everyone knows they are already cooked—a simple pen marking on the egg works.

For scrambled eggs "Egg Beaters" or "Liquid Egg Whites" are also great options if you like them. They are very compact, quick, and easy to use. For easy clean-up, use nonstick oil spray on the skillet in addition to butter or oil before you add the scrambled eggs, and cook them to the desired doneness. The same goes for sunny side up eggs.

A "microwave egg cooker" may be a great investment if you have only one or two people on board who like eggs. Breakfast will be ready in one to two minutes, and clean-up is also quick. Some recipes using microwave egg cookers are provided on page 105, 106 and 109.

The only downside to eggs is that egg cartons take up a lot of space in the refrigerator. If your group likes eggs, start with a maximum of two dozen, and buy more along the way. They are easy to find in local stores and even bakeries along your sailing routes.

We have already touched on why bacon is not a boat-friendly food in Chapter 1 and that bacon bits are much more convenient. They are sold in 8-ounce pouches or 4-ounce plastic bottles. They are easy to pack, ready to use, and easily stored at cabin temperature due to the high salt content. You can sprinkle them on top of scrambled eggs, omelets, or salads.

Fully cooked breakfast sausages are also convenient since they can be heated in the microwave, but, just like bacon, they can create a lingering smell.

OVERNIGHT OATS

This is my favorite way to make oatmeal on the boat. I can throw this together during dinner prep the night before so it's ready the next morning. It can keep in the fridge for up to three days. It's creamy, delicious, and cold and hits the spot in the warm climate. If GF, bring gluten-free oats from home.

Makes 6 Servings (V–a, VGT, DF–a, GF–a)

 **INGREDIENTS**

- 3 cups rolled oats
- 3 cups milk (almond, coconut, or regular)
- 3 teaspoons honey or sugar (optional)
- ½ cup raisins (optional)
- ½ cup nuts (optional)
- Dash of cinnamon (optional)

 **PREPARATION**

1. Put all of the ingredients into a container with a lid and let it sit overnight in the refrigerator.
2. Serve by itself, or add yogurt, peanut butter, chia seeds, fresh banana, or frozen berries.

PEANUT BUTTER BANANA WRAP

A classic combo in an easy-to-eat wrap

Makes 1 Serving (V, DF)

 **INGREDIENTS**

2   tablespoons peanut
     butter
1   8-inch tortilla
1   tablespoon jelly, jam, or
     honey
½   banana, sliced
1   tablespoon granola or
     sunflower seeds

 **PREPARATION**

1.   Spread the peanut butter on the
     tortilla, and add the toppings.
2.   Roll it up, and cut it in half.

NEVENA MRDALJ

AVOCADO TOAST

Check your avocadoes every morning and when they begin to soften, they will be perfect for this easy breakfast.

Makes 1 Serving (V, DF)

INGREDIENTS

½   avocado, halved, pitted, and mashed in its skin

1   slice of bread, toasted
Salt and pepper

Topping Options:

Squeeze of lime juice

Dash of hot sauce

Tomatoes, radishes, cucumber slices

PREPARATION

1.   Spread the mashed avocado over the toast.

2.   Sprinkle with salt and pepper, and add toppings of choice.

CITRUS SALAD

This combination of fruits is light and refreshing, especially when chilled. If you want to serve the whole group, combine the canned fruits the night before and add bananas in the morning.

Makes 6 Cups (V, DF, GF)

 **INGREDIENTS**

 **PREPARATION**

2   14-ounce cans grapefruit segments, drained

1   20-ounce can pineapple chunks, drained, but liquid reserved

1   10-ounce can mandarin segments, drained

1   6-ounce jar Maraschino cherries (optional)

2   bananas, sliced

1.   Combine all ingredients (including the optional cherries) except for the bananas in a bowl with a lid.

2.   Mix gently and refrigerate for several hours or overnight.

3.   Add sliced bananas right before serving.

QUINOA CUP

Loaded with protein, this breakfast will keep you full all morning.

Makes 1 Serving (VGT, GF)

 **INGREDIENTS**

½   cup cooked quinoa (page 215)

½   cup yogurt

1   tablespoon peanut butter

½   banana, sliced

1   teaspoon chia seeds

1   teaspoon honey

PREPARATION

1.   Add all ingredients to a cup.

2.   Serve immediately.

YOGURT BERRY PARFAIT

Enjoy this cool parfait while the soft rays of the morning sun are casting a glow all around you.

Makes 1 Serving (VGT, GF-a)

 **INGREDIENTS**

½ cup frozen strawberries or mixed berries

½ cup yogurt

3 tablespoons granola

 **PREPARATION**

1. Add the frozen berries to a cup.
2. Top with yogurt and granola.

MANGO BANANA SMOOTHIE

More than forty varieties of mangoes grow in the Virgin Islands. Once a taxi driver gave us half a dozen freshly picked mangoes instead of change. They were delicious!

Makes 20 Ounces (V, DF, GF)

 **INGREDIENTS**

 **PREPARATION**

INGREDIENTS	PREPARATION
1 banana, frozen	1. Put all ingredients in the blender.
1 cup mango chunks, fresh or frozen	2. Process until smooth.
1½ cups orange juice	

BERRY PASSION SMOOTHIE

Passion fruit trees are scattered all over the Virgin Islands. If you have never had passion fruit juice, try some. It has a distinct flavor that goes nicely with berries.

Makes 20 Ounces (V, DF, GF)

 **INGREDIENTS**

1   banana, frozen, peeled and cubed

1   cup mixed berries, frozen

1½   cups passion fruit juice

 **PREPARATION**

1. Put all ingredients in the blender.
2. Process until smooth.

GREEN ENERGY BOOST SMOOTHIE

Have a cold smoothie after a morning hike or swim. Mixes of various frozen fruits and veggies such as kale or spinach can be bought. Depending on how filling and how sweet you want your smoothie to be, you can either add water, any type of milk, or juice.

Makes 16 Ounces (V, DF, GF)

 **INGREDIENTS**

1   8-ounce pouch of fruit and vegetables

1   cup of water, milk, or juice

2   ice cubes

1   tablespoon of sugar or honey (optional)

1   tablespoon of ground flaxseed (optional)

 **PREPARATION**

1.   Put all ingredients in the blender.

2.   Process until smooth.

PAPAYA SMOOTHIE

Papaya also grows locally. You can buy it fresh or frozen. Frozen papaya is usually harvested at the peak of ripeness, and it is already peeled and cut up. This smoothie always tastes like it is an essential part of island living.

Makes 16 Ounces (V, DF, GF)

 **INGREDIENTS**

 **PREPARATION**

1   cup coconut milk

1   frozen banana, partially thawed

1   cup papaya chunks, frozen or fresh

1   tablespoon sugar

6   ice cubes (optional)

1. Combine coconut milk, banana, papaya, and sugar in the blender.
2. Blend until smooth.
3. Add ice cubes and process again until frothy.

SOURSOP PINEAPPLE SMOOTHIE

Soursop is a local fruit that is healthy and delicious. If you come across it, buy some to try. It is ripe when you can easily punch the skin with your finger. Soursop comes in different sizes, and you will get several servings from one fruit. The recipe below gives proportions based on two cups of soursop flesh. Adjust quantity of pineapple and juice according to how big your soursop is. Removing the seeds of the soursop can be time-consuming, so enlist help.

Makes 32 Ounces (V, DF, GF)

 ### INGREDIENTS

 ### PREPARATION

1	medium soursop (yields about 2 cups soursop flesh)
1½	cups pineapple chunks, fresh, canned, or frozen
2	cups pineapple juice

1. Cut soursop in half, then into wedges. Remove the skin and the black seeds.
2. Put soursop in the blender.
3. Add pineapple chunks and pineapple juice.
4. Blend until smooth and refrigerate if needed to chill before drinking.

STRAWBERRY YOGURT SMOOTHIE

A classic smoothie you can enjoy anytime and anywhere on deck.

Makes 20 Ounces (VGT, GF)

 **INGREDIENTS**

 **PREPARATION**

1	cup strawberries, frozen
½	banana, frozen or fresh
½	cup milk (any kind)
2	teaspoons honey or sugar
1	teaspoon ground flaxseed (optional)
1	cup yogurt

1. Combine all ingredients except for yogurt in a blender. Blend until smooth.

2. Add yogurt and blend for 1 more minute. If it's too thick, add a little bit more milk to make a creamy consistency.

NEVENA MRDALJ

MEDITERRANEAN EGGWHITES

This healthy breakfast comes together in a few minutes from start to finish.

Makes 1 Serving (VGT)

 **INGREDIENTS**

 **PREPARATION**

2	egg whites
¼	cup fresh spinach, chopped or 1 tablespoon frozen spinach, thawed
3	grape tomatoes, chopped
1	ounce feta cheese crumbles
1	English muffin, cut in half, toasted

1. Add egg whites, spinach, tomatoes, and feta cheese to a microwave egg cooker.

2. Stir, close the cover, and cook in the microwave for 1 to 2 minutes until fully cooked.

3. Serve cooked egg whites on top of English muffin.

EGG BREAKFAST BURRITO

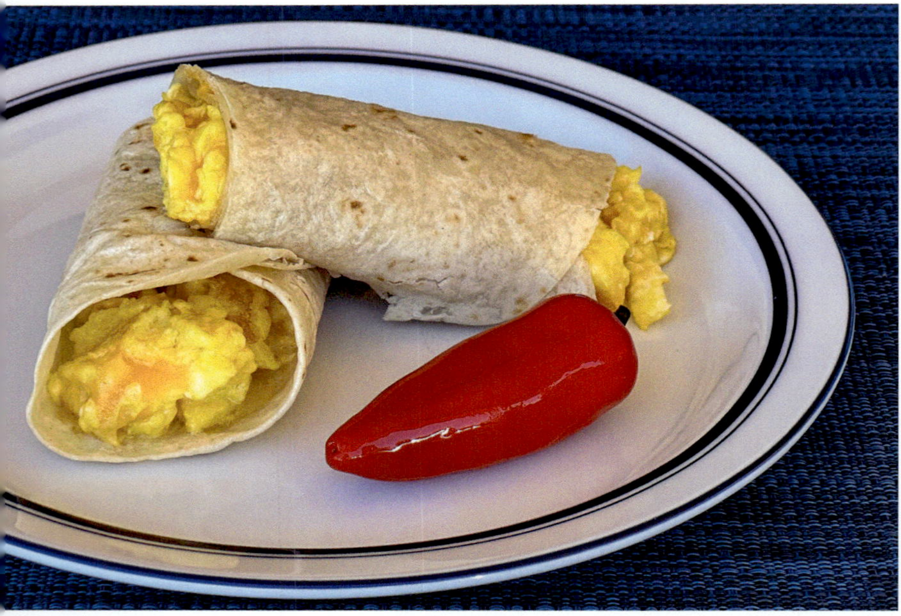

Makes 1 Serving (VGT)

 **INGREDIENTS**

 **PREPARATION**

2	eggs
1	slice of cheese (optional)
1	tortilla
2	tablespoons cooked black beans (optional)
	Salt and pepper to taste
	Salsa or hot sauce (optional)

1. Crack eggs into microwave egg cooker and stir with a fork to break the yolk.
2. Close cover and cook in the microwave for 1 to 2 minutes.
3. Add cheese and cook for 30 more seconds.
4. Place the cooked eggs onto a tortilla, add the desired toppings, and roll up.

BREAKFAST SKILLETS

A hearty breakfast which puts leftover boiled potatoes or grilled veggies to good use and gets everyone ready for a fun-filled day.

Makes 1 to 4 Servings per skillet (VGT or M)

 **INGREDIENTS**

For each serving you will need:

Oil or butter, for coating pan

¼ cup boiled potatoes, diced

¼ cup grilled or fresh veggies, diced

⅛ cup ham, diced

1-3 eggs

1 tablespoon of shredded cheese of your choice (optional)

1 tablespoon dash of bacon bits (optional)

 **PREPARATION**

1. Heat a skillet and coat with nonstick spray and/or some oil or butter.

2. Add cut up boiled potatoes, veggies and/or ham, and sauté for 2 to 3 minutes.

3. Crack eggs on top of the vegetables and/or meat, stir, and cover with a lid.

4. Cook to the desired doneness, stirring if necessary, usually 2 to 3 minutes longer.

5. Add shredded cheese and bacon bits before serving, if desired.

TOFU SCRAMBLE

A good option for vegan sailors.

Makes 2 Servings (V, GF)

 **INGREDIENTS**

6 ounces firm tofu, drained, pressed dry and cubed

1 teaspoon salt

1 teaspoon ground turmeric

½ teaspoon garlic powder

3 tablespoons oil

½ onion, chopped

1 red, green or yellow pepper, chopped

1 cup plant-based sausage crumbles (optional)

1 can (4 ounces) sliced mushrooms, drained (optional)

Black pepper for garnish (optional)

2 tablespoons green herbs for garnish (optional)

6 corn tortillas

 **PREPARATION**

1. Combine tofu with spices in a bowl.

2. Heat oil in a pan and sauté onions, peppers, and frozen sausage crumbles until soft.

3. Add the optional mushrooms and the tofu mixture to the pan and cook for 5 to 7 minutes.

4. Garnish with black pepper and parsley or cilantro.

5. Serve with corn tortillas.

POACHED EGG AND AVOCADO

Makes 1 Serving (VGT)

 **INGREDIENTS**

 **PREPARATION**

1	egg
½	teaspoon water
½	avocado, sliced
½	bagel, toasted
	Salt and pepper to taste

1. Crack egg into microwave egg cooker and pour water over the egg. Close cover and cook for 30 seconds. Add 15 to 30 more seconds if needed.

2. Place avocado slices on the toasted bagel half, then top with the poached egg. Season with salt and pepper.

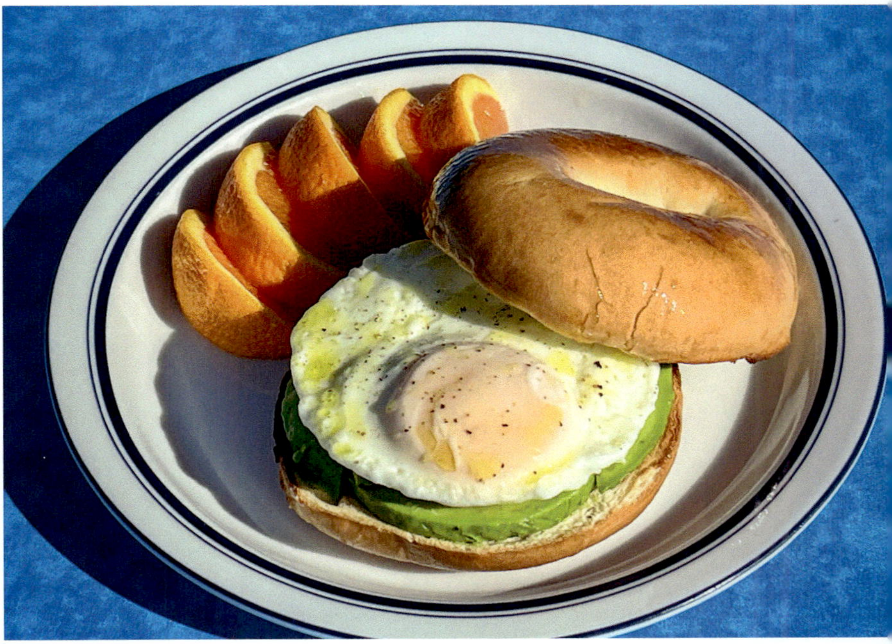

CHAPTER 8

SNACKS AND APPETIZERS

Snacking on a yacht in the Caribbean is all about fresh, flavorful, and light bites that are easy to enjoy between water activities or while lounging in your favorite spot on the boat. Snacks are in high demand and should be treated as a fourth meal for planning purposes. All snacks that do not require refrigeration are easy to find and restock, especially chips, pretzels, nuts, and popcorn. Corn chips, salsa, and ready-made guacamole go well with beer. You can make your own trail mix by combining equal parts of salted peanuts, M&Ms, and raisins. Chilled pudding cups can satisfy a craving for sweets or have an apple with peanut butter. Here are a few more snacks and appetizers you can try.

MEXICAN DIP

After an afternoon of kayaking and exploration, you will need something substantial to satiate your hunger. This may fit the bill.

Makes 6 Servings (VGT, GF)

 **INGREDIENTS**

1	16-ounce can vegetarian refried beans
1	cup chunky salsa
2	cups plain yogurt or sour cream
2	tablespoons cilantro, chopped
1	cup shredded Cheddar cheese or Mexican style blend
1	3-ounce can black olives, sliced
1	jalapeño, seeded and sliced (optional)
1	11-ounce bag of corn tortilla chips

 **PREPARATION**

1. Combine refried beans with ⅓ cup salsa, and spread the mixture into the serving dish.
2. Add the yogurt and the cilantro on top of the beans.
3. Spread the remaining salsa, followed by the shredded Cheddar cheese.
4. Top with black olives and jalapeno slices.
5. Serve with corn tortilla chips.

NEVENA MRDALJ

HUMMUS AND VEGGIES

When you need to replenish your energy after snorkeling around the reefs, reach for this dip and your favorite carbs. Ready-made, packaged hummus is usually available in various flavors.

Makes 6 Servings (V, DF, GF-a)

 **INGREDIENTS**

1. 10-ounce container of hummus
2. handfuls of your choice of celery sticks, baby carrots, green or red bell peppers (cut-up), fresh zucchini sticks, cucumber rounds, or crackers

 **PREPARATION**

1. Arrange hummus and optional dipping items on a large plate.
2. Serve crackers on the side.

EGGS WITH SMOKED SALMON

Smoked salmon on top of eggs and crackers is perfect for those who need a satisfying snack in the late afternoon. Classic deviled eggs are hard to arrange on a plate on a rocky boat. This version has all the same ingredients but is easier to make and a bit more stable on the serving platter.

Makes 6 Servings (F, DF)

 **INGREDIENTS**

6 tablespoons mayonnaise

2 teaspoons Dijon mustard

1 teaspoon dried dill, divided (optional)

30 crackers of your choice

6 hard-boiled eggs, peeled and sliced into 30 rounds

2 ounces smoked salmon slices, finely chopped

1 stalk green onion, finely chopped (optional)

Salt and paprika or pepper, to taste

 **PREPARATION**

1. Combine mayonnaise, mustard, and half of the dill and spread onto the crackers.

2. Arrange the crackers on a plate and top with egg slices.

3. Add the salmon bits on top of the egg slices.

4. Sprinkle the remaining dill or green onion on top.

5. Add salt and paprika or pepper according to taste.

CELERY WITH BOURSIN

This is so simple, yet it tastes like it belongs on a yacht. A perfect mix of texture and flavor.

Makes 6 Servings (VGT, GF)

 **INGREDIENTS**

 **PREPARATION**

1   Boursin cheese, softened

6   celery ribs, cut into 3-inch pieces

1.   Spread the cheese on the celery sticks.

2.   Arrange on a plate.

SHRIMP COCKTAIL

Chilled, tender shrimp with the zesty sauce is a refreshing, savory appetizer
that makes each bite feel like a celebration of the sea.

Makes 6 Servings (SF, DF, GF)

 **INGREDIENTS**

1   10-ounce jar cocktail sauce for seafood

1   pound frozen cooked shrimp

1½   lemons, cut into 6 quarters

 **PREPARATION**

1. Place frozen shrimp in a bowl of cold water and let thaw for 20 minutes.

2. Drain well, gently squeeze the shrimp to remove any excess water, and pat dry with paper towels.

3. Divide the cocktail sauce amongst 6 serving cups.

4. Add 4 to 5 shrimp to each cup, and garnish with the lemon quarters.

CHEESE AND CUCUMBER BITES

A simple spread of cheese and crackers accompanied by fruit or vegetables becomes a memorable picnic on the deck, especially when paired with a chilled glass of wine.

Makes 6 Servings (VGT, GF-a)

 **INGREDIENTS**

12	ounces of assorted cheeses – precut into squares.
30	crackers
1	English cucumber cut into 30 rounds
1	3-ounce can black olives, sliced
¼	red pepper, thinly sliced for garnish (optional)

 **PREPARATION**

1. Stack crackers, cheese and cucumber slices.
2. Arrange on plate and top with black olives and red pepper slices.
3. Omit crackers if gluten-free.

MEZZE PLATTER

A combination of savory and salty delicacies, which pairs well with wine or beer to help you rehydrate after a day in the sun.

Makes 6 Servings (GF-a)

 **INGREDIENTS**

 **PREPARATION**

6	ounces cured meats, such as prosciuttos, salami, chorizo
6	ounces cheese, assorted
1	cup nuts
½	cup dried fruit (optional)
8	ounces crackers, assorted
½	cup mixed olives (optional)

1. Arrange cured meats, cheeses, nuts, crackers, olives, and dried fruit on a cutting board.
2. Substitute veggies for crackers if gluten-free.

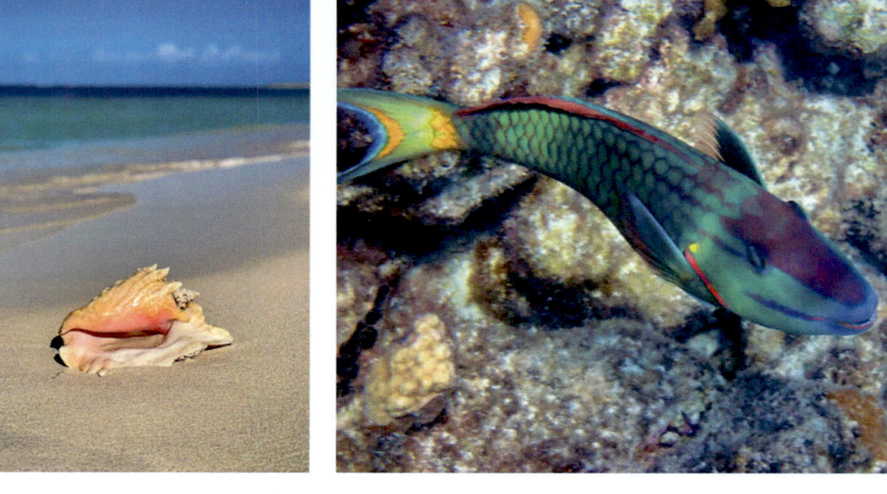

CHAPTER 9

SANDWICHES AND SOUPS

I know that everyone knows how to make a sandwich, but everyone makes it their own way. Some sandwich options are listed here because people often forget about condiments and because it is beneficial to see the variety of ingredients in one spot when compiling the grocery list and planning quantities. Survey your group and see how they prepare their sandwiches and what they like.

Canned soups seem very convenient for the boat; if you like to eat hot soups, then by all means, put some on your grocery list. But be mindful of the warm weather. Hot soup is not as appealing in the Caribbean Sea as it is in the Great Lakes. I used to always have cans of soup left over at the end of every trip. Now I only make cold soups. If you like soup, try the Gazpacho or the Avocado Soup on pages 130 and 129. They both take less than 10 minutes to prepare.

HAM AND CHEESE SANDWICH

A typical sandwich in an atypical setting. Prepare it and enjoy it while you are sailing. It will be a whole new experience.

Makes 1 Serving (M)

 **INGREDIENTS**

1	tablespoon mayo or butter
1	teaspoon mustard
1	sandwich roll
6	slices of ham (4 ounces)
2	slices of cheese (2 ounces)
1	lettuce leaf, cut in half (optional)

 **PREPARATION**

1. Spread condiments on each side of the roll.
2. Add all the desired ingredients.

TURKEY AVOCADO POCKET

Creamy avocadoes combined with turkey is a perfect combination for a mid-day meal on the sea.

Makes 1 Serving (P, DF)

 **INGREDIENTS**

 **PREPARATION**

2	teaspoons mayo
1	pita bread
6	slices of turkey breast (4 ounces)
2	small lettuce leaves (optional)
1	medium avocado, cut into slices
	Salt and pepper to taste

1. Cut pita bread in half and spread mayo inside each pita pocket.
2. Insert turkey slices, lettuce, and avocado.

TUNA SALAD

The flavor of the tuna pairs beautifully with the salty air. It's almost as easy to prepare tuna salad for six people as it is for one.

Makes 6 Servings (F, DF, GF-a)

 ### INGREDIENTS

 ### PREPARATION

4	5-ounce cans of tuna, drained
4	tablespoons mayo or more
2	teaspoons Dijon mustard (optional)
2	stalks of celery, diced
1	carrot, diced (optional)
½	medium red onion, finely chopped (optional)
	Salt and pepper to taste
12	slices of bread

1. Flake the tuna with a fork in a bowl.
2. Add all the other desired ingredients and mix well.
3. Put tuna salad between 2 slices of bread.

VEGGIE WRAP

Fresh veggies or grilled veggies, your favorite cheese and dressing—veggie sandwiches and wraps are so versatile. Add a piece of fruit and some crunchy chips, and your meal is complete.

Makes 1 Serving (P, DF)

 ### INGREDIENTS

 ### PREPARATION

2	cheese slices (2 ounces)
1	lettuce leaf
1	medium tomato, sliced
½	carrot, sliced into rounds
½	zucchini, sliced into rounds
¼	medium red onion, sliced thin
1	8-inch tortilla
4	tablespoons Ranch dressing

1. Arrange cheese, lettuce, tomatoes, carrots, zucchini, and red onions on tortilla.

2. Top with Ranch dressing, roll up, and cut in half.

LOX BAGEL

Smoked salmon is easy to find, and a little bit goes a long way. The rich, smokey flavor of the salmon will taste better on a yacht than it would at any upscale deli.

Makes 1 Serving (F)

 **INGREDIENTS**

 **PREPARATION**

1	bagel, sliced in half
2	tablespoons of cream cheese
2	ounces smoked salmon slices
1	lettuce leaf
1	medium tomato, sliced
⅛	medium red onion, sliced thin

1. Toast bagel.
2. Spread cream cheese on the bagel halves.
3. Add smoked salmon, lettuce, tomato and onion.

NEVENA MRDALJ

EGG SALAD

Making egg salad for the whole group is a breeze when you already have hardboiled eggs on hand. Get help with peeling and chopping, and lunch will be ready in minutes.

Makes 6 Servings (VGT)

 **INGREDIENTS**

⅔ cup mayonnaise

2 teaspoons Dijon mustard (optional)

3 tablespoons celery, finely chopped

6 eggs, hardboiled and chopped

Salt and pepper, to taste

6 pita breads, cut in half

 **PREPARATION**

1. Mix the mayo, mustard, and celery in a bowl.

2. Add chopped hardboiled eggs.

3. Sprinkle with salt and pepper, and serve in pita bread pockets.

QUESADILLA

A warm tortilla filled with melted cheese of your choice will taste just right when you are surrounded by turquoise waters, no matter how you prepare it: on the grill, in a skillet, or in the microwave.

Makes 1 Serving (VGT)

 **INGREDIENTS**

1	8-inch tortilla
¼	cup shredded cheese, such as Colby Jack, Mexican style blend or Cheddar
2	tablespoons salsa (optional)
2	tablespoons sour cream (optional)

 **PREPARATION**

1. Put the tortilla on a preheated grill for about 1 to 3 minutes until the bottom side is slightly charred.
2. Flip over, add the cheese to one half of the tortilla, and fold over the other half.
3. Grill for 1 to 2 minutes until cheese melts, flipping over again if necessary.
4. Serve with salsa, sour cream, or your favorite sides.

NEVENA MRDALJ

AVOCADO SOUP

This soup is very filling and well-suited for those with a big appetite. After a long swim you just may need an energy boost.

Makes 6 cups (VGT, GF)

 **INGREDIENTS**

4	Hass avocados, medium, cut in half
4	teaspoons fresh lemon juice
2	cups plain full-fat yogurt
2	teaspoons salt
½	teaspoon black pepper
1	cup parsley or cilantro, chopped
2	cups salsa, ready-made

 **PREPARATION**

1. Put 2 cups of water, scooped out avocado chunks, lemon juice, yogurt, salt and pepper in the blender. Save some parsley/cilantro for garnish.

2. Blend on high for 2 minutes or until the consistency is smooth. If too thick, add a little bit more water.

3. Add the salsa and chopped parsley/cilantro, saving about 2 tablespoons for garnish, and stir it in by hand.

4. Refrigerate for 1 to 3 hours to let the flavors blend.

5. Stir again before serving and garnish each soup bowl or cup with the remaining parsley/cilantro.

GAZPACHO

Make it in the morning and have it for lunch at midday when it is hot. You can even serve it in plastic cups and eliminate washing dishes. Just don't mistake them for Bloody Mary's.

Makes 6 cups (VGT, V–a, GF–a)

 **INGREDIENTS**

1½	green pepper
1½	yellow pepper
1½	cup parsley
6	garlic cloves
3	15-ounce cans tomatoes, diced
¾	cup olive oil
3	tablespoons red wine vinegar
	Salt and pepper, to taste
6	teaspoons sour cream (optional)
1½	cup croutons (optional)

NEVENA MRDALJ

PREPARATION

1. Chop peppers, parsley, and garlic into big chunks, and put them into the blender.
2. Add the canned tomatoes with their juice, oil, and vinegar, and blend for 2 minutes.
3. Season with salt and black pepper, and refrigerate for 2 hours to let the flavors blend.
4. Serve with a dollop of sour cream and croutons, if desired.

CHAPTER 10

COLD DISHES

Most of the dishes presented in this section are high in protein and very filling. Some contain chicken or cured meats, others contain shrimp and tuna, and the rest derive their protein source from legumes. Adding extra sources of protein is also easy. You can serve them as a main course, as a side dish, or even as an appetizer, depending upon the quantity served and the accompaniments. Therefore, I measure the yields in terms of number of cups, and you can adjust the quantities how you see fit. They are extremely convenient for preparation because they utilize the stovetop minimally or not at all. What this means is that you don't need to run the generator in order to prepare them, which takes out one step of the planning process of when to cook food on a boat. If a generator is needed, the timing is flexible, and quickly cooking some pasta or boiling shrimp (if you couldn't buy ready-to-eat frozen shrimp) can be done in the morning while coffee and breakfast are being prepared. I present many options for cold dishes in order to accommodate a wide variety of dietary preferences. Most of these recipes also taste best when chilled, so they can be made ahead of time and enjoyed whenever your group gets hungry.

CHICKEN WALDORF SALAD

Makes 6 cups (P, VGT-a, GF-a)

INGREDIENTS

¾	cup mayonnaise	1	cup grapes, sliced in half or ¼
¾	cup yogurt		cup of raisins or Craisins
3	tablespoons lemon juice	1	cup apples, cubed
	Salt and pepper, to taste	1	cup walnuts, chopped
3	cups chicken breast, grilled	6	pita breads or 9 ounces of
1	cup celery, thinly sliced		crackers

PREPARATION

1. Combine mayonnaise, yogurt, lemon juice, and salt and pepper in a serving bowl, and whisk well.
2. Add all the other ingredients and stir to coat well.
3. Refrigerate for 2 hours and for up to 2 days.
4. Serve with pita bread or crackers.
5. If vegetarian, omit the chicken. If gluten-free, omit the pita bread/ crackers.

ANTIPASTO SALAD

Combine sunshine, pasta, beans, and crunchy vegetables. Add some cured meats and cheeses, and your meal will be complete.

Makes 14 cups (M, VGT-a)

 NEVENA MRDALJ

INGREDIENTS

1	16-ounce box pasta, penne or farfalle
2	teaspoons of salt
1	15-ounce can cannellini, or white beans
½	yellow pepper, chopped
1	carrot, sliced
½	green pepper, chopped
½	red onion, sliced
½	cup green or black olives
1	cup Italian salad dressing
4	ounces of feta cheese, cut into cubes
6	ounces of salami or prosciutto
6	ounces of Parmesan cheese

PREPARATION

1. Bring 4 quarts of water to boil in a large pot, add salt and the pasta, and cook according to package directions, stirring occasionally.
2. While the pasta is cooking, pick a large bowl with a lid. Put the beans and all the vegetables in the bottom of the bowl. Add the salad dressing.
3. When the pasta is cooked al dente, drain it, rinse it with 2 cups of cold water and let it cool for another 10 minutes.
4. Add the cooled pasta to the vegetables, mix well, and cover the bowl.
5. Refrigerate for a couple of hours for the flavors to blend.
6. Before serving add the feta cheese and cured meats and mix again.
7. Top with Parmesan cheese once it is plated.

PINEAPPLE CHICKEN SLAW

A healthy salad with a tropical flavor. Perfect for a sunny day on the water.

Makes 9 to 10 cups (P, VGT–a, GF)

INGREDIENTS

Salad:

1	20-ounce can pineapple chunks, drained but liquid reserved
1	medium head of red or green cabbage, thinly sliced (yields 10—12 cups initially, but it will wilt)
1	carrot, sliced
½	cup slivered or sliced almonds
3	green onions, sliced

Dressing:

¾	cup of mayonnaise
4	tablespoons apple cider or white vinegar
6	tablespoons pineapple juice, reserved from drained pineapple chunks
2	teaspoons salt
½	teaspoon cracked black pepper
3	cups chicken breast, grilled and cubed

PREPARATION

1. Mix all salad ingredients together in a large bowl with a lid.
2. Mix all the dressing ingredients together in the measuring cup or a separate bowl.
3. Pour the dressing on the salad and mix until well-coated.
4. Refrigerate for 1-2 hours until ready to serve.
5. Top with grilled chicken. Best if eaten the same day.

CAJUN SHRIMP

A go-to appetizer for potluck dinners on land, and a main event for sunset dinners on deck.

Makes 6 to 7 cups (SF, GF)

 **INGREDIENTS**

Shrimp:

2	pounds frozen cooked shrimp

Sauce:

6	tablespoons mayonnaise
6	tablespoons ketchup
2	garlic cloves, pressed

1	lemon, juiced
2	teaspoons seafood seasoning
1	dash of cayenne pepper
1	dash of hot sauce, or more if you like it spicy
4	green onions

 **PREPARATION**

1. Place frozen shrimp in a bowl of cold water and let thaw for 20 minutes.
2. Meanwhile, combine the first seven ingredients in a large bowl and mix well to make the sauce.
3. Slice green onions diagonally and add to sauce. Add hot sauce to taste.
4. Once thawed, drain the shrimp well, gently squeezing it to remove any excess water, and pat dry with paper towels.
5. Add shrimp to the sauce and mix well.
6. Refrigerate for at least 2 hours to combine flavors, stirring a couple of times. This can be prepared up to 6 hours in advance.

TUNA AND WHITE BEAN SALAD

A common appetizer along the Mediterranean coast in Portugal, Spain and Italy and now a protein-packed option for lunch in the Caribbean waters.

Makes 8 to 9 cups (F, DF, GF)

INGREDIENTS

Dressing:

6   tablespoons lemon juice

6   tablespoons olive oil

2   teaspoons salt

½   teaspoon cracked black pepper

Vegetables:

1   English cucumber, cubed

½   cup parsley, chopped

½   onion, chopped

1   3-ounce can black olives or Kalamata olives, sliced (optional)

½   red pepper, finely chopped

Beans and Tuna:

2   15-ounce cans cannellini, butter beans, or small white beans, drained and rinsed

4   5-ounce albacore tuna, drained

3   pita breads cut in half or 6 to 9 ounces of crackers

PREPARATION

1. Mix the dressing ingredients in a large bowl with a lid.
2. Add the vegetables to the vinaigrette and mix.
3. Add beans and tuna, gently combining everything.
4. Refrigerate 2 to 4 hours for flavors to blend.
5. Serve with pita bread or crackers.

SHRIMP AND AVOCADO SALAD

You can never go wrong with a shrimp and avocado combination. A simple but delicious meal you can share and enjoy with your group accompanied by your favorite drinks.

Makes 8 to 9 cups (SF, DF, GF)

INGREDIENTS

Salad:

2	pounds frozen cooked shrimp
2	15-ounce cans corn, whole kernel, drained
1	15-ounce can diced tomatoes, well-drained
¼	cup cilantro, chopped
2	avocadoes, cut into ½-inch cubes

Dressing:

½	cup olive oil
½	cup fresh lime juice from 1 to 2 limes
½	teaspoon salt
¼	teaspoon pepper

PREPARATION

1. Place frozen shrimp in a bowl of cold water and let thaw for 20 minutes.
2. Meanwhile, whisk together the dressing ingredients in a large bowl.
3. Once thawed, drain the shrimp well, gently squeezing it to remove any excess water, and pat dry with paper towels.
4. Add the corn, tomatoes, shrimp, and cilantro to the dressing and mix well.
5. Refrigerate for 2 hours or more.
6. Add the avocado cubes just before serving.

DEVILED SHRIMP

The tangy shrimp in combination with the beautiful surroundings elevates the entire dining experience.

Makes 6 to 8 cups (SF, DF, GF)

# INGREDIENTS

2	pounds frozen cooked shrimp		1	lemon, washed, cut in half lengthwise, then thinly sliced with skin on
½	cup fresh lemon juice			
¼	cup olive oil			
1	tablespoon red wine vinegar		1	small red onion, thinly sliced
1	garlic clove, finely diced		1	3-ounce can black olives, sliced, well-drained
1	bay leaf, broken up			
1	tablespoon dry mustard		4	tablespoons red pepper, finely chopped
¼	teaspoon cayenne pepper			
1	teaspoon salt		1	baguette, 6 to 9 ounces of pita chips or a vegetarian pasta salad as a side
¼	teaspoon black pepper			

PREPARATION

1. Place frozen shrimp in a bowl of cold water and let thaw for 20 minutes.
2. Meanwhile, combine lemon juice, oil, vinegar, spices, and herbs, and whisk them together.
3. Add the lemon, onion, black olives, and red pepper.
4. Once thawed, drain the shrimp well, gently squeezing it to remove any excess water, and pat dry with paper towels.
5. Add the shrimp, and gently mix to coat the shrimp with the marinade.
6. Cover the dish, and refrigerate for at least 2 hours, stirring it once or twice.
7. Serve with a baguette, pita chips or a vegetarian pasta salad.

ANEGADA LOBSTER SALAD

Anegada lobster is a Caribbean delicacy, particularly famous on the island of Anegada in the BVI. The lobsters have long, spiny antennae, and their meat is tender, sweet, and flavorful when grilled. When making a dinner reservation, you must specify ahead of time what size lobster you want for your meal. If you can't quite finish it, bring the leftovers back to the boat, and make a lobster salad for lunch the next day. This recipe also works well with canned crab meat.

Makes 1 to 2 cups (SF, DF, GF-a)

INGREDIENTS

1	stalk of celery, finely chopped		2	tablespoons mayonnaise
¼	cup red onion, chopped and lightly salted		2	tablespoons lime juice
				Salt, to taste
1	tablespoon parsley, chopped (optional)		1	cup grilled lobster chunks
			1	bun, piece of toast or lettuce

PREPARATION

1. Mix everything except for the lobster chunks together.
2. Add the lobster chunks, and put in the refrigerator for 20 to 30 minutes for the flavors to blend.
3. Serve on a bun, on some lettuce, or on a piece of toast.

NICOISE SALAD

In France, this salad is often enjoyed during warm weather, and, therefore, it's ideal for enjoying on a yacht. The recipe lists quantities for individual plates and servings.

Makes 1 Serving (F, DF, GF)

 **INGREDIENTS**

1	5-ounce can tuna	¼	cup green olives
1	egg, hard-boiled, peeled, and cubed	3	tablespoons salad dressing (vinaigrette or Italian)
8	ounces canned green beans	1	teaspoon Dijon mustard
½	cup boiled potatoes		

 **PREPARATION**

1. Arrange tuna, egg and vegetables separately on each individual plate.
2. Mix a vinaigrette or Italian dressing with the Dijon mustard.
3. Drizzle dressing over each of the components and enjoy the various textures.

TUNA WITH GREEN BEANS

This is so easy to prepare and, yet, surprisingly good. All the main ingredients are shelf-stable and could be used for an unplanned, quick meal if need be.

Makes 6 to 8 cups (F, DF, GF)

INGREDIENTS

3	15-ounce cans green beans, chilled and drained		4	5-ounce cans tuna, chilled and drained
3	15-ounce cans diced tomatoes, chilled and drained		3	tablespoons capers (optional)
1½	cups sliced black olives (optional)		3	medium lemons, juiced
			6	tablespoons olive oil
				Salt and pepper, to taste

PREPARATION

1. Divide green beans, tomatoes, olives, tuna, and capers amongst individual plates.
2. Drizzle the lemon juice and olive oil on top, and mix gently.

CARIBBEAN QUINOA SALAD

The flavor of the Jerk seasoning combined with the tangy mango reminds
your palate that you are in a relaxed and sunny atmosphere.

Makes 7 to 8 cups (V, DF, GF)

 **INGREDIENTS**

1 cup quinoa, uncooked

Lime Jerk Dressing:

2 tablespoons lime juice

1 tablespoon honey

1 teaspoon Dijon mustard

2 teaspoons Jerk seasoning

4 tablespoons olive oil

Salt and pepper, to taste

Salad:

1 15-ounce can black beans, drained and rinsed

½ red bell pepper, chopped

½ green pepper, chopped

1 mango, peeled and cubed

1 8-ounce can corn, drained and rinsed

½ cup red onion, chopped

¼ cup parsley, chopped (optional)

Salt and pepper, to taste

 **PREPARATION**

1. Cook the quinoa according to package directions, or instructions on page 215. Let it cool completely. You will have 3-3 ½ cups of cooked quinoa. This can be done the night before.
2. Whisk all the dressing ingredients in a large serving bowl.
3. Add quinoa, the vegetables, and the herbs and spices, and toss gently.
4. Serve immediately or refrigerate. It will keep in the refrigerator for 2 to 3 days.

BLACK BEAN SALAD

A classic dish from the Southwest and a perfect side for chicken, beef or fish in the tropics, as well.

Makes 7 to 8 cups (V, DF, GF)

 **INGREDIENTS**

1	medium lime, juiced
½	cup fresh cilantro, finely chopped
1	tablespoon ground cumin
½	cup of olive oil
2	garlic cloves, finely chopped (optional)
1	small red pepper, chopped
½	small red onion, chopped

	Salt and pepper, to taste
2	15-ounce cans black beans, drained and rinsed
1	15-ounce can diced tomatoes, drained
1	8-ounce can corn, drained
2	avocados, cubed (optional)
	Dash of hot sauce, according to taste

 **PREPARATION**

1. Combine lime juice, cilantro, cumin, oil, chopped garlic, peppers, onions, salt and pepper in a large bowl.
2. Add black beans, tomatoes, and corn, and mix well.
3. Refrigerate for 2 to 3 hours to let the flavors combine. The salad can be kept in the refrigerator for a couple of days.
4. Garnish with avocado cubes just before serving and hot sauce according to taste.

LENTIL SALAD

Canned lentils are easier to digest than beans for some individuals, so here is a recipe with an Italian twist. Do we have any Chianti on board?

Makes 4 to 5 cups (V, DF, GF)

 NEVENA MRDALJ

 **INGREDIENTS**

Dressing:

¼	cup balsamic or red wine vinegar
½	cup olive oil
4	garlic cloves, minced
2	teaspoons salt

Salad:

2	15-ounce cans cooked lentils, drained and rinsed
1	14-ounce can diced tomatoes, drained
½	cup celery, finely chopped
½	cup red onion, chopped
½	cup parsley, chopped
½	cup green onions, sliced

PREPARATION

1. Whisk together the dressing ingredients in a large serving bowl.

2. Add lentils, tomatoes, celery, red onion, parsley, and green onions.

3. Toss gently to coat and refrigerate for a couple of hours.

VEGGIE PASTA SALAD

A colorful medley of al dente pasta and vibrant vegetables tossed in a zesty salad dressing. A simple meal, perfect for lunch or dinner, or with your favorite meat.

Makes 12 cups (V, DF)

 NEVENA MRDALJ

INGREDIENTS

1	16-ounce box pasta, such as penne or farfalle
2	teaspoons salt
1	medium cucumber, cubed
1	large carrot, sliced
½	red pepper, chopped
½	green pepper, chopped
8	ounces zesty Italian salad dressing

PREPARATION

1. Bring 4 quarts of water to boil in a large pot, add salt and the pasta, and cook according to package directions, stirring occasionally.
2. Put the prepared vegetables in the bottom of a large bowl with a lid.
3. Add the salad dressing and let the vegetables marinate.
4. When the pasta is cooked al dente, drain it, rinse it with 2 cups of cold water and let it cool for 10 minutes.
5. Add the pasta to the vegetables, mix well, and cover the bowl.
6. Refrigerate the salad and mix again before serving.

RAMEN NOODLE SALAD

Almost everyone loves ramen noodles. Enjoy them in a cold salad that
brings a taste of home into the beauty of the open sea.

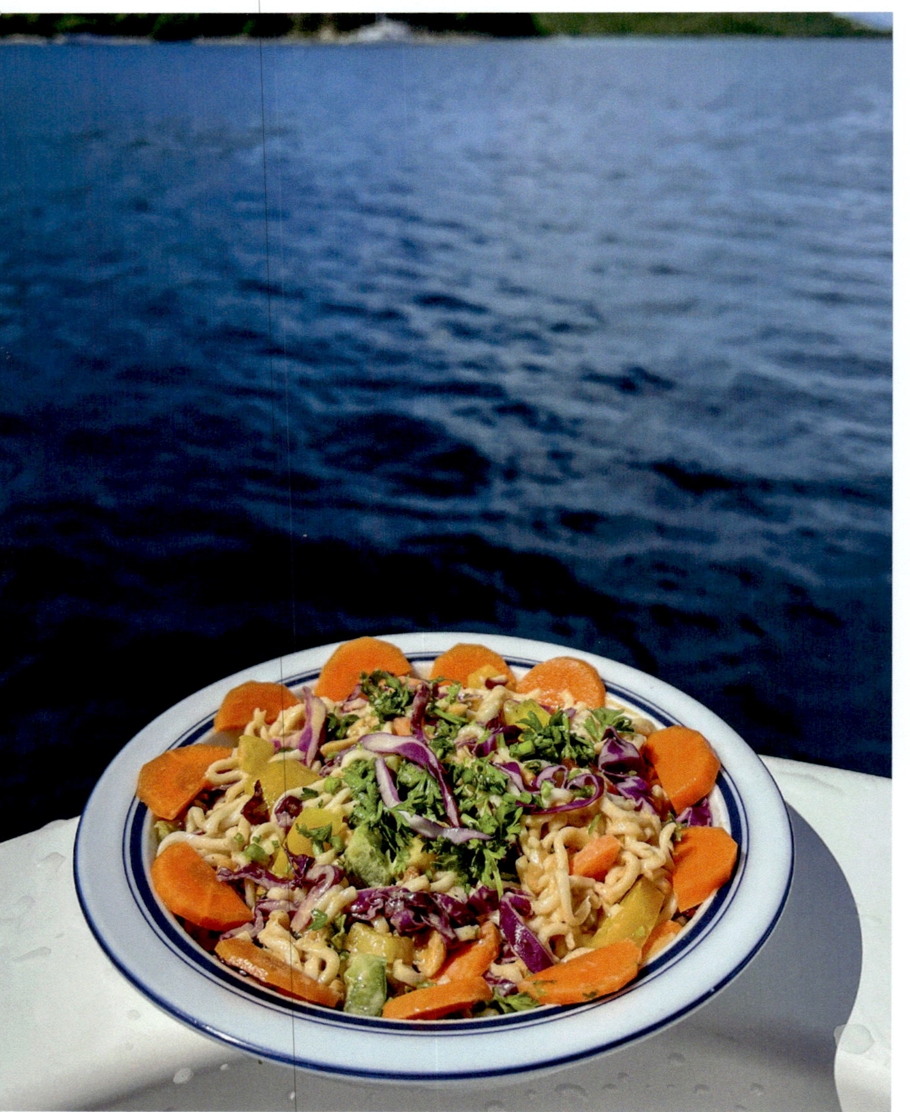

Makes 6 to 8 cups (V, DF)

 NEVENA MRDALJ

 **INGREDIENTS**

2	3-ounce ramen noodle packets

Salad:

2	cups red cabbage, thinly sliced
1	cup carrots, sliced
1	cup yellow pepper, sliced
1	cup green pepper, sliced
1	cup bean sprouts (optional)
¼	cup parsley, chopped
½	cup peanuts

 **Dressing:**

½	cup creamy peanut butter
½	cup canola oil
2	tablespoons soy sauce
2	tablespoons lime juice
1	tablespoon sugar
1	tablespoon hot sauce

PREPARATION

1. Put both packets of Ramen noodles in a bowl and add 2 to 3 cups of boiling water to cover them. Let sit for 5 minutes. Rinse with cold water and drain well.
2. Whisk all dressing ingredients in a large bowl.
3. Add the cold noodles and all the vegetables to the bowl, except for the parsley and peanuts.
4. Mix well to coat and combine.
5. Serve immediately or chill in the refrigerator.
6. Top with parsley and peanuts before serving.

CHICKPEA MACARONI SALAD

Makes 7 cups (V, DF)

 **INGREDIENTS**

2	cups elbow macaroni, uncooked
1	teaspoon salt

Dressing:

3	tablespoons red wine vinegar
4	teaspoons fresh lemon juice
1	tablespoon dried mint
1	tablespoon dried basil
6	tablespoons olive oil
	Salt, to taste

Salad:

1	15-ounce can garbanzo beans, drained and rinsed
½	red onion, finely chopped
1	cup grape tomatoes, whole (optional)
	Salt and pepper, to taste

 **PREPARATION**

1. Bring 2 quarts of water to boil in a large pot, add salt and the macaroni, and cook according to package directions, stirring occasionally.
2. Whisk all the dressing ingredients in a large serving bowl.
3. When the macaroni are cooked al dente, drain them, rinse with 2 cups of cold water, and let them cool for 10 minutes.
4. Add the garbanzo beans, cooked macaroni, and vegetables to the bowl and toss gently.
5. Serve immediately or refrigerate. It will keep in the refrigerator for 2 to 3 days.

MIXED BEAN SALAD

This recipe from a Randall's Mixed Beans jar and has been one of my favorites for many years. In the Caribbean, cans of white and pink beans are available and make a good substitute for the beans in the original recipe.

Makes 8 to 9 cups (V, DF, GF)

NEVENA MRDALJ

 **INGREDIENTS**

1	15-ounce can white beans	1	cucumber peeled, seeded, and chopped
2	10-ounce cans pink beans		
1	cup celery, chopped	½	cup parsley, chopped
1	cup carrots, sliced	¾	cup Italian dressing or vinaigrette
1	green pepper, chopped		
1	cup onion, chopped		

 **PREPARATION**

1. Pour beans into a strainer, rinse with water, and drain well.
2. Combine beans with veggies in a large bowl.
3. Add parsley.
4. Toss with Italian dressing or vinaigrette.

CHAPTER 11

FROM THE STOVETOP

Cooking on a stovetop is quicker than cooking in an oven and, depending on what type of grill your boat has, it also can be much quicker than grilling. You can sauté vegetables, boil hot dogs, or sear chicken breasts, sausages, pork tenderloin rounds, or burger patties. Tofu, if first pressed, can be pan-seared, as well. The amount of time needed to cook a particular meat will vary upon the thickness of the cut, the amount of heat used, and the type of cookware, so a meat thermometer comes in handy.

JERK CHICKEN FAJITAS

A mix of bold, tropical flavors that feel perfectly suited to the laid-back vibe of a yacht. You can substitute beef, pork tenderloin, or shrimp for the chicken.

Makes 6 Servings (P, DF-a, GF-a)

 **INGREDIENTS**

1½	pounds chicken breast, boneless, skinless	1	medium green pepper, seeded and cut into strips
1	lime, juiced		Salt and pepper, to taste
2	teaspoons Caribbean Jerk seasoning, divided	6	8-inch tortillas
6	tablespoons oil, divided	1	cup shredded Cheddar cheese
2	medium onions, sliced	6	tablespoons salsa (optional)
2	medium red peppers, seeded and cut into strips	6	tablespoons sour cream (optional)
		6	tablespoons guacamole (optional)

 **PREPARATION**

1. Cut chicken breast meat into strips, and put the meat with the lime juice into a zip-close bag to marinate for at least 30 minutes and up to 24 hours.
2. Before cooking the meat, drain the liquid from the bag, pat it dry a bit and season the meat with 1 teaspoon of jerk seasoning.
3. Heat oil in a large skillet, and cook chicken strips until cooked through, about 12 minutes, stirring frequently. Chicken will be done when the juices run clear when pierced with a fork or the meat temperature reaches 165°F.
4. Transfer to a plate and set aside.
5. Add more oil to the skillet if necessary and add the onions and peppers. Cook them over high heat until they start to soften, about 5 to 6 minutes. Add the remaining jerk seasoning, and salt and pepper to taste.
6. Return the cooked chicken strips to the skillet and combine with the vegetables. Serve immediately with tortillas, cheese, and toppings. If gluten-free, omit the tortilla and serve with rice or beans, if dairy-free omit the sour cream and cheese.

PASTA WITH MEATBALLS

Preparing a basic pasta dish in the boat's galley creates a homemade charm enhanced by the unique experience of boat life.

Makes 6 Servings (M, DF-a, V-a)

NEVENA MRDALJ

INGREDIENTS

1	16-ounce box spaghetti, penne or farfalle		1½	pounds frozen meatballs (beef, pork, chicken, plant-based)
1	teaspoon salt		½	cup Parmesan cheese (optional)
3	teaspoons olive oil			Dash of crushed red peppers (optional)
1	24-ounce jar spaghetti sauce			

PREPARATION

1. Bring 4 quarts of water to boil in a large pot, add salt and the pasta, and cook according to package directions, stirring occasionally.
2. While the pasta is cooking, heat oil in a large skillet over medium-high heat and add a jar of pasta sauce.
3. Add frozen meatballs to the sauce, cover the skillet to avoid splattering, and cook until the meatballs are defrosted and cooked thoroughly, about 10 to 15 minutes or until they reach an internal temperature of 165°F.
4. When the pasta is al dente, drain it, and either place the cooked pasta directly into the pan with the meatballs, tossing gently to combine or serve the two separately.
5. Add a sprinkle of Parmesan cheese and crushed red pepper, if desired.

PAN-SEARED CHICKEN

Searing boneless chicken breasts in a pan creates delicious browning on the outside while sealing in the juices. You can add any vegetables you like. The Herbs de Provence seasoning gives it a sophisticated flavor, which complements the yachting experience.

Serves 6 (P, DF, GF)

 **INGREDIENTS**

3 pounds chicken breasts, boneless, skinless

3 tablespoons Herbs de Provence seasoning

Salt and pepper, to taste

Oil or nonstick cooking spray for the pan

 **PREPARATION**

1. Rinse chicken breasts and pat dry with paper towels.
2. Arrange them on a plate and season both sides with the seasoning, the salt, and the pepper.
3. Heat the oil in a large skillet on medium heat, and add the chicken.
4. Cook until slightly golden on both sides and juices run clear when pierced with a fork, about 10 to 15 minutes. The internal temperature should be at least 165°F.
5. Serve with favorite sides. Refrigerate leftovers for additions to salads.

PESTO SHRIMP

The orange glow of the setting sun makes a nice backdrop to the colors in this dish. Pause for a minute to fully take in the beauty all around you.

Makes 6 Servings (SF, DF-a)

 **INGREDIENTS**

1	16-ounce box pasta, linguini, penne or farfalle	1	10-ounce bag frozen broccoli
1	teaspoon salt	1	14-ounce can diced tomatoes
3	tablespoons olive oil	6	tablespoons ready-made pesto
2	pounds frozen raw shrimp, peeled, deveined, and thawed		Salt and pepper, to taste
		½	cup Parmesan cheese (optional)

 **PREPARATION**

1. Place frozen shrimp in a bowl of cold water and let thaw for 20 minutes.
2. Bring 4 quarts of water to boil in a large pot, add salt and the pasta, and cook according to package directions, stirring occasionally.
3. Drain the shrimp well, gently squeezing it to remove any excess water, and pat dry with paper towels.
4. While pasta is cooking, heat oil in a large skillet and sauté shrimp for 2 to 4 minutes until shrimp is pink on both sides. Remove shrimp from skillet.
5. Add frozen broccoli to the same skillet, and cook it covered for 3 to 4 minutes.
6. Add tomatoes and pesto sauce and cook for 5 more minutes.
7. When vegetables are heated thoroughly, return the sauteed shrimp to the pan and mix to combine.
8. When the pasta is al dente, drain it, and either place the cooked pasta directly into the pan with the shrimp mixture, tossing gently to combine or serve the two separately.
9. Top with Parmesan cheese, if desired.

LENTIL BOLOGNESE

A classic dish that will satisfy any vegan sailors aboard.

Don't forget the red wine!

Makes 6 cups (V, DF, GF)

 **INGREDIENTS**

- 3 tablespoons oil
- ¾ cup onion, diced
- 3 garlic cloves, minced
- 2 4-ounce cans sliced mushrooms
- 1 teaspoon Italian seasoning
- ½ teaspoon red pepper flakes
- 1 14-ounce can fire-roasted diced tomatoes, drained
- 1 24-ounce jar marinara sauce
- 1 15-ounce can cooked lentils, drained
- ⅓ cup red wine (optional)
- Salt and pepper, to taste
- 6 to 9 cups cooked pasta or cooked spaghetti squash

PREPARATION

1. Heat the olive oil in a pan, add the onions, garlic, mushrooms, Italian seasoning, and red pepper flakes and sauté for 5 to 10 minutes.
2. Add the tomatoes, marinara sauce, and lentils and simmer for 15 minutes.
3. Add the red wine, and cook for 5 more minutes.
4. Serve over cooked pasta or spaghetti squash.

ARTICHOKE PASTA

As you savor the Mediterranean-inspired flavors in this dish and listen to sounds of the sea, relax and enjoy the company of the people you are with.

Makes 6 Servings (V, DF, GF)

 **INGREDIENTS**

1	16-ounce box of pasta—linguini, farfalle or penne	3	14-ounce cans diced tomatoes, drained
1	teaspoon salt	1	cup Kalamata or black olives, sliced
6	tablespoons of oil	1½	teaspoons Italian seasoning
4	teaspoons minced garlic		Salt and pepper, to taste
3	14-ounce cans quartered artichoke hearts, drained	½	cup or more Parmesan cheese (optional)

 **PREPARATION**

1. Bring 4 quarts of water to boil in a large pot, add salt and the pasta, and cook according to package directions, stirring occasionally.
2. While the pasta is cooking, heat the oil in a large skillet, add garlic, and sauté 1 to 2 minutes.
3. Add the artichokes, diced tomatoes, olives and Italian seasoning and cook for 5 to 7 minutes or until heated thoroughly.
4. Add salt and black pepper according to taste.
5. When the pasta is al dente, drain it and either place the cooked pasta directly into the pan with the vegetable sauce, tossing gently to combine or serve the two separately.
6. Top with Parmesan cheese, if desired.

WHITE BEANS AND SPINACH

An adaptation from an old Italian recipe called "Beans and Greens." A main meal for vegans, and a great side dish for grilled Italian sausages.

Makes 6 Servings (V, DF, GF-a)

INGREDIENTS

6	tablespoons oil		1	vegetable bouillon dissolved in 2 cups of water or 2 cups of vegetable broth
1	teaspoon crushed red pepper flakes			
4	cloves of garlic, finely chopped		3	15-ounce cans cannellini, northern or white beans, drained and rinsed
3	10-ounce packages frozen chopped spinach			Salt and pepper, to taste
			1	baguette or 6 rolls (optional)

PREPARATION

1. Heat the oil over medium heat in a large saucepan. Add pepper flakes and garlic and sauté both for about 2 minutes until garlic becomes fragrant and golden.
2. Add frozen spinach, cover the pan, lower the heat, and let the spinach thaw. Stir every 2 minutes until thawed.
3. Add 1 cup of vegetable broth, reduce the heat to a simmer, and let cook for about 10 minutes.
4. Add the beans and stir to combine. Add more broth if needed so that everything can simmer for another 3–5 minutes, letting the flavors come together.
5. Season with salt and pepper to taste and serve with a baguette or rolls.

CHAPTER 12

FROM THE GRILL

Grilling on a boat is fun. You can cool off in the water while waiting for the coals or the grill to heat up. Everyone is mulling around getting the meat, vegetables, and condiments ready. The smell of the charcoal combined with the sea breeze and the plopping sounds of the pelicans as they catch their dinner from the sea is a new experience. You will be grilling with a drink in one hand, just like at home, but this setting is so much better!

If you are a grill master at home, do not expect to have a fancy grill aboard. Your experience combined with the information you will gather from the charter company before you arrive should help you determine if you want to grill at all. Gas, charcoal, and electric grills all have their own pros and cons, and your group's experience level with a particular type of grill should determine what type of food you want to grill. You will need to preheat the grill properly, for at least ten to twelve minutes, to prevent food from sticking. If using a charcoal grill, let the coals burn until covered with white ash before putting food on the grates. Also using oil or nonstick cooking spray on the food directly will make grilling easier. Marinades with some sugar, such as salad dressings, honey, or teriyaki sauce, will caramelize and give meat, fish, and tofu grill marks and some crispiness on the outside. The recipes presented here are very basic, and a meat thermometer is always helpful to determine the doneness of the meat or fish.

BURGERS

Burgers are almost everyone's favorites and perfect for cooking on a boat. They cook quickly and come in so many different varieties. You can buy ground beef patties, salmon burgers, veggie burgers, or grill portabella mushrooms. You can add any cheese you like or have them plain. Everyone can add the condiments and sides of their choosing and enjoy a simple and familiar meal.

Makes 6 Servings (M, DF-a, VGT-a)

 **INGREDIENTS**

3	pounds ground meat 80/20 or burger patties (frozen or fresh) Salt and pepper, to taste Olive oil, vegetable oil or nonstick cooking spray
6	hamburger buns Cheese slices (optional)

Optional condiments: mustard, ketchup, mayonnaise, lettuce, tomatoes, onion, jalapeños, pickles, hot peppers, relish, steak sauce

 **PREPARATION**

1. Defrost burger patties or shape 8 ounces of ground beef into patties that are all about the same size and about ¾-inch thick.
2. Season with salt and pepper. Brush the burger patties with oil on both sides, and place them on the preheated grill.
3. Grill the burger patties over direct medium heat for 8 to 10 minutes, turning them over after 4 to 5 minutes. Burgers will be done when the internal temperature reaches 160°F or the meat is still pink in the center for medium doneness. Adjust the cooking time by minus 2 minutes for rare or plus 2 minutes for well-done.
4. For the last 30 seconds, add sliced hamburger buns to the grill to lightly toast them. For cheeseburgers, add a slice of cheese to each burger and let it melt.
5. Serve burgers with condiments of your choice.

STEAK

Enjoying a juicy steak aboard your charter yacht is a balance of elegance and simplicity – fine dining while you are nestled in a tranquil anchorage.

Makes 6 Servings (M, DF, GF)

INGREDIENTS

4	pounds of beef steak: rib-eye, sirloin, New York strip, beef tenderloin (1-inch thick or about 8 to 12 ounces per steak)	Salt and black pepper, to taste
		Olive oil, vegetable oil or nonstick cooking spray
	1	bottle of steak sauce

PREPARATION

1. Season both sides of the steaks with salt and pepper.
2. Let them sit at cabin temperature for about 15 minutes.
3. Preheat the grill.
4. Brush both sides of the steaks with oil.
5. Grill the steaks over direct medium heat until the internal temperature reaches the desired doneness, about 8 to 14 minutes, turning them over once at the midpoint.

   Medium Rare: 140°F or 4 to 5 minutes on each side

   Medium: 150°F or 5 to 6 minutes on each side

   Well Done: 160°F or 6 to 7 minutes on each side
6. Remove from the grill, cover with aluminum foil, and let the steaks rest for about 3 minutes before eating.
7. Serve with your favorite steak sauce and sides.

GRILLED CHICKEN BREAST

On a yacht grilled chicken tastes light, but satisfying, perfect for a main entrée with sides or as a topping to various salads.

Makes 6 Servings (P, DF, GF)

 **INGREDIENTS**

3	pounds chicken breasts, boneless, skinless		1	cup Italian salad dressing (or marinade of your choice)
	Salt and pepper, to taste			Olive oil, vegetable oil, or nonstick cooking spray

 **PREPARATION**

1. Rinse chicken breasts with cold water, and pat dry with paper towels.
2. Season with salt and pepper, then put in a large resealable freezer bag with the salad dressing or marinade of your choice.
3. Refrigerate and marinate for at least 30 minutes and up to 2 days.
4. Preheat the grill to medium heat.
5. Remove the chicken from the bag and discard the marinade. Pat the meat dry with paper towels.
6. Lightly brush or spray with oil on both sides.
7. Grill the chicken breasts over direct medium heat for 8 to 10 minutes, turning them over after 4 to 5 minutes. The chicken will be done when pierced with a fork, the juices run clear, and the meat is no longer pink in the center, or an internal temperature of 165°F.

HERBED PORK TENDERLOIN

The juicy, tender meat and the flavors of the subtle herbs are perfectly suited to the elegant setting and the endless horizon around you.

Makes 6 Servings (M, DF, GF)

 **INGREDIENTS**

3	tablespoons Herbs de Provence
1	teaspoon salt
½	teaspoon black pepper
1	teaspoon garlic powder

3	pounds pork tenderloin
3	tablespoons of oil
	Olive oil, vegetable oil or nonstick cooking spray

 **PREPARATION**

1. Mix the seasoning, and rub onto the tenderloins. You can also swap out the seasoning for Chicago Steak seasoning.
2. Coat the tenderloins with oil, and put them in a resealable plastic bag.
3. Refrigerate and marinate for at least 30 minutes and up to 2 days, turning once or twice.
4. Allow to stand at cabin temperature for 15 minutes before grilling.
5. Preheat the grill to medium heat.
6. Lightly brush or spray more oil on all sides of the meat if needed before placing on grill.
7. Grill over indirect medium heat for 30 minutes, turning once after 15 minutes. The internal temperature should reach 160°F or until the juices run clear when pierced with the tip of a knife.
8. Remove from the grill, cover with aluminum foil, and let stand for 5–10 minutes so that the internal juices of the meat get absorbed before slicing.

HOT DOGS AND SAUSAGES

So many possibilities! A picnic on a boat and fun for all! Nowadays even far away from home you can find hot dogs and sausages that are plant-based or made with chicken or turkey in addition to traditional ones made with beef and pork.

Makes 6 Servings (M, P, VGT-a)

 **INGREDIENTS**

6 to 12 hot dogs or sausages,
depending on your party size
6 to 12 hot dog buns, depending on
your party size
Olive oil, vegetable oil or nonstick
cooking spray

Optional condiments: mustard,
ketchup, relish, shredded cheese,
canned chili sauce, pickles,
onions

 **PREPARATION**

1. Preheat the grill to medium heat and lightly brush or spray some oil on the hot dogs or sausages.
2. Grill hot dogs and sausages over indirect medium heat according to package directions or an internal temperature of 165°F. Sausages are usually done when the juices run clear if pierced with the tip of a knife.
3. For the last 30 seconds, add sliced hot dog buns to the grill to lightly toast them.
4. Serve with condiments of your choice and side dishes.

PITA PIZZAS

While pizza is served in many restaurants, one can make individual pizzas with pita bread on the boat as well. For each individual 8-inch pizza you will need the following ingredients.

Makes 1 Serving (M, VGT-a)

 **INGREDIENTS**

2	tablespoons of sauce: pizza, tomato, spaghetti, or pesto
1	pita bread, whole wheat or white
¼	cup shredded mozzarella or Parmesan cheese
2	ounces of meat: pepperoni slices, chopped ham, cooked ground beef
2	ounces of vegetables: olives, mushrooms, peppers, onions, zucchini
	Italian seasoning (optional)
	Red pepper flakes (optional)
	Parmesan cheese (optional)

 **PREPARATION**

1. Preheat the grill to medium heat.
2. Assemble each individual pizza by spreading a thin layer of sauce on one pita bread, followed by the cheese, meat, vegetables, and Italian seasoning.
3. Grill on direct medium heat with the grill cover closed until vegetables are soft and cheese is melted.
4. Top with red pepper flakes and Parmesan cheese, if desired.

COCONUT SHRIMP

Coconut shrimp combines food from the sea with fruit from tropical islands,
a perfect pairing for a delightful dinner while you're floating on a boat.

Makes 6 Servings (SF, DF)

INGREDIENTS

6	garlic cloves, finely chopped		2	tablespoons dried basil leaves
¼	cup soy sauce		1	lime, cut into quarters
¼	cup oil			Salt, to taste
2	pounds raw shrimp, peeled, deveined, preferably with tails left on (not frozen)			1 or 2 skewers per person (optional) Olive oil, vegetable oil or nonstick cooking spray
½	cup unsweetened shredded coconut, plus more for serving			

PREPARATION

1. Combine garlic, soy sauce, and ¼ cup oil with the shrimp in a resealable plastic bag. Place bag in refrigerator and let the shrimp marinate for 5 to 30 minutes.
2. Grilling shrimp on skewers is optional, but easier. Bring some skewers from home. Soak them in water for 10 to 30 minutes beforehand so they don't catch on fire.
3. Preheat the grill to medium heat.
4. Discard the marinade from the bag, and add the coconut flakes to bag, shaking the bag to coat the shrimp.
5. Arrange the shrimp in an even layer on the grate or skewer them, and brush lightly with oil. Grill them over direct high heat. Turn them after about one minute and continue grilling until shrimp turns pink, opaque, and lightly charred, 1–2 more minutes. Total cooking time is 2–4 minutes.
6. Transfer to individual plates and top shrimp with dried basil, squeezed lime juice, salt, and more coconut.
7. Serve with desired sides.

MAHI-MAHI WITH SALSA VERDE

Mahi-mahi, a local favorite, is known for its firm, lean texture and mild flavor. As the fish sizzles on the grill, it takes on a beautiful char that adds a subtle smokiness. Serving it with an olive-oil based salsa will ensure that it stays moist.

Makes 6 Servings (F, DF, GF)

NEVENA MRDALJ

 **INGREDIENTS**

Fish:

2 to 3 pounds mahi-mahi fillets

Olive oil, vegetable oil, or
nonstick cooking spray

1 teaspoon salt

¼ cup olive oil

Salsa Verde:

3 tablespoons minced garlic

1½ cup finely chopped fresh parsley

¾ cup olive oil

1 teaspoon salt

White Wine Marinade:

½ cup white wine

2 tablespoons Seafood or
Caribbean Jerk seasoning

 **PREPARATION**

1. Combine the marinade ingredients in a resealable plastic bag. Add the thawed filets to the bag, seal it and place in the refrigerator. After 20 to 30 minutes, remove the filets from the bag and discard the marinade.
2. Preheat the grill to medium-high heat.
3. To prepare the Salsa Verde, put all the ingredients in the blender and pulse several times or finely chop by hand and combine. Set aside.
4. Brush or spray the seasoned marinated fish filets with oil on both sides and place them on the preheated grill.
5. Grill over direct high heat for 7 to 9 minutes total, turning once after 4 minutes. Fish will be done when the flesh is opaque and separates easily with a fork or the internal temperature reaches 145°F.
6. Top the fillets with the Salsa Verde and serve with your favorite sides.

RED SNAPPER WITH MANGO SALSA

Grilled snapper melts in your mouth with just the right balance of citrus brightness and natural sweetness, a dish that celebrates the sea's bounty in an authentic way.

Makes 6 Servings (F, DF, GF)

 NEVENA MRDALJ

 **INGREDIENTS**

Fish:

2 to 3 pounds of red snapper fillets

Olive oil, vegetable oil, or nonstick cooking spray

Lemon Marinade:

1 whole lemon, juiced

¼ cup olive oil

Salt and pepper

Mango Salsa:

2 cups mango chunks, fresh or frozen

2 jalapeños or ½ green pepper, seeded and minced

1 cup red onion, finely diced

6 tablespoons lime juice

6 tablespoons olive oil

1 teaspoon salt

2 tablespoons cilantro, finely chopped and divided

½ teaspoon red pepper flakes, if not using jalapeño

 **PREPARATION**

1. Add marinade ingredients to a resealable plastic bag. Add the fillets to the lemon marinade, seal the bag and place it in the refrigerator. After 20 to 30 minutes, remove the fillets from the bag and discard the marinade.

2. To prepare the Mango Salsa, place all ingredients (minus some cilantro) in a bowl. Mix well to blend. Cover and refrigerate until ready to serve.

3. Preheat the grill to medium-high heat.

4. Brush or spray the seasoned marinated fish filets with olive oil on both sides and place them on the preheated grill.

5. Grill over direct high heat for 7 to 9 minutes total, turning once after 4 minutes. Fish will be done when the flesh is opaque and it separates easily with a fork, or the internal temperature reaches 145°F.

6. To serve, top with Mango Salsa and the remaining cilantro, and add your favorite sides.

SEASONED SALMON

Having grilled salmon in the Caribbean brings together the rich, buttery flavors of the fish and the warmth of the tropics. A true delight.

Makes 6 Servings (F, DF, GF)

INGREDIENTS

Fish:

2 to 3 pounds of salmon fillets

Olive oil, vegetable oil, or
nonstick cooking spray

Soy Sauce Marinade:

6 tablespoons soy sauce

6 tablespoons oil

1 teaspoon garlic powder

1 teaspoon salt

PREPARATION

1. Put marinade ingredients into a resealable plastic bag. Add the salmon fillets to the marinade and place in the refrigerator for 20 to 30 minutes. Remove the filets from the bag and discard the marinade.
2. Preheat the grill to medium-high heat.
3. Season, brush the flesh side of the fillets with oil, and place them, skin side down, on the preheated grill.
4. Grill fillets over direct high heat for 7 to 8 minutes or until you can lift them off with a spatula without the fish sticking to the grill grates. Turn them over and cook for another 2 to 4 minutes depending on the thickness of the filet. Check for doneness, making sure the flesh in the middle is opaque and separates easily with a fork or the internal temperature reaches 145°F.
5. Serve warm with favorite sides.

GRILLED TOFU WITH CHIMICHURRI

Grilled tofu is a light, refreshing plant-based protein that complements the gentle breeze on deck. Choose your favorite marinade and grill to create a crispy exterior. Serve it with a vibrant Chimichurri sauce and your favorite vegetables.

Makes 6 Servings (V, DF)

NEVENA MRDALJ

INGREDIENTS

Tofu:

2   16-ounce packages firm or extra firm tofu

1   cup of marinade (salad dressing of your choice or teriyaki sauce)
Olive oil, vegetable oil, or nonstick cooking spray

Chimichurri:

2   cups parsley, very coarsely chopped

¾   cup olive oil

1   tablespoon dried oregano

6   tablespoons red wine vinegar

4   garlic cloves, quartered

1   teaspoon salt

½   teaspoon pepper

½   teaspoon crushed red pepper flakes

PREPARATION

1.   To remove the water that is naturally in tofu, wrap each slice into 2 pieces of paper towel, put on a plate, and put something heavy on top so it presses out all the extra water. Leave like that for at least 30 minutes.

2.   Marinate the tofu in your favorite marinade for about 30 minutes.

3.   Make the Chimichurri sauce while the tofu is marinating. Put all the ingredients in a blender and pulse until the ingredients are minced.

4.   Preheat the grill to medium heat.

5.   Brush the tofu with oil or cooking spray and grill it over direct heat for 3 to 5 minutes on each side, occasionally brushing with extra marinade. There is no way to undercook tofu. It is done when it has nice grill marks and is crispy on the outside.

6.   Serve the tofu with Chimichurri sauce and your favorite sides.

CAULIFLOWER STEAK

Surrounded by the open sea, eating grilled cauliflower steaks paired
with hummus and pesto can feel like a perfect fusion of simplicity and
sophistication for those who eat a lighter fare.

Makes 2 to 3 Servings (V, DF, GF)

 **INGREDIENTS**

1	head of cauliflower (yields 2-3 steaks)	4-6	tablespoons ready-made basil pesto
	Olive oil, vegetable oil or nonstick cooking spray	3-9	tablespoons ready-made hummus
	Salt and pepper		

 **PREPARATION**

1. Trim and wash the head of cauliflower and cut to size 2-3 steaks.
2. Preheat the grill to medium heat
3. Brush or spray both sides with oil and season with salt and pepper.
4. Grill on direct medium heat until the steaks have grill marks and are tender, about 4 to 6 minutes per side.
5. Serve with ready-made pesto and hummus.

CHAPTER 13

EASY SIDES

Rice and potatoes are classic sides that most people like and are able to eat. We have already talked about my challenges with rice in "Food and Galley Tips" on page 65 and why I only use precooked rice pouches. Similarly, I am a big fan of instant mashed potatoes pouches where a mere 4 ounces is enough for two people. These products are hit-and-miss in local stores on the islands, so I ask each couple to bring one pouch with them if we decide that we want rice or mashed potatoes as a side dish for one meal. Other favorites include mac and cheese, baked or refried beans in cans, and frozen broccoli or vegetable mixes in microwave-safe bags. Boiling red skin potatoes in salted water for about 20 minutes or until they are tender and serving them with butter is also easy. A few other very simple sides are listed in this section.

ADRIATIC POTATO SALAD

As you enjoy this tangy potato salad on a boat, surrounded by sparkling blue waters, each forkful feels cooling and refreshing.

Makes 6 Servings (V, DF, GF)

 **INGREDIENTS**

Potatoes:

2   pounds potatoes, peeled if necessary, and sliced thin into rounds

1   tablespoon salt

Dressing:

4   tablespoons lemon juice

4   tablespoons apple cider vinegar

½   cup olive oil

1   teaspoon salt

½   teaspoon black pepper

1   cup onions, white or red, sliced thin

½   cup parsley, finely chopped

PREPARATION

1.   Wash potatoes, and cut them into slices to speed up the cooking process.

2.   Put the potatoes in a saucepan, and add salt and enough water to cover them. Cook the potatoes for 20 to 25 minutes until they are tender when pierced with the tip of a knife, but not falling apart. Drain in a colander.

3.   Whisk together the dressing ingredients in a small bowl, then add the chopped onions and parsley.

4.   In a serving container with a lid, arrange one layer of cooked potato slices, then spoon some of the dressing with the onions and parsley on top. Potatoes should still be warm, but not hot. Repeat with as many layers as necessary.

5.   Refrigerate or let sit at cabin temperature for 2 hours before serving.

SPICY CORN

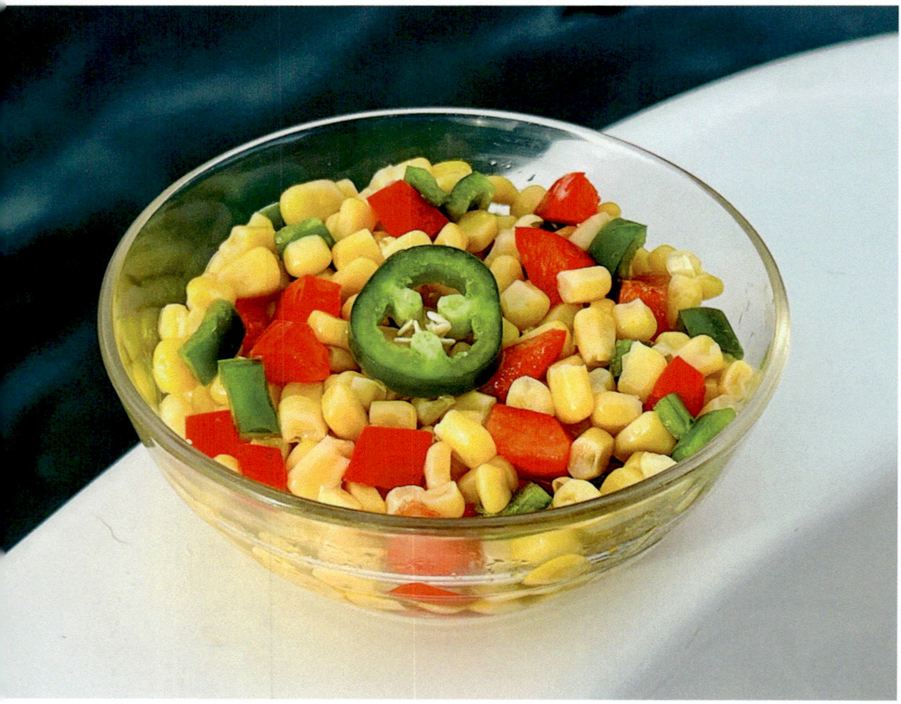

Makes 6 Servings (V-a, VGT, DF-a, GF)

 **INGREDIENTS**

 **PREPARATION**

3   15-ounce cans corn, whole kernel, drained

4   tablespoons butter or olive oil

1   red pepper, diced

1   jalapeño, seeded and finely diced

½   teaspoon garlic powder

Squeeze of lime juice (optional)

1. Combine all the ingredients in a bowl.

2. Heat in the microwave for 3 to 5 minutes.

NEVENA MRDALJ

QUINOA

Serve this fluffy, nutty grain instead of rice because it is much easier to cook. It takes on the flavor of any spice or topping you add to it.

Makes 6 Servings (V, GF)

 **INGREDIENTS**

2 cups quinoa

3½ cups water, chicken broth or coconut milk

Salt, to taste

2 tablespoons butter (optional)

Chimichurri (page 207, optional)

Mango Salsa (page 203, optional)

Salsa Verde (page 201)

1 15-ounce can black beans (optional)

 **PREPARATION**

1. Combine quinoa, water, broth, or coconut milk in a pot.

2. Add salt if needed and bring to a rolling boil.

3. Reduce heat, cover, and simmer until liquid has evaporated, about 15 minutes.

4. Let stand for 5 minutes, then fluff with a fork.

5. Combine with your favorite toppings, such as Salsa Verde, Chimichurri or Mango Salsa when serving as a side dish.

6. Cooked quinoa will keep in the refrigerator for 3 to 4 days.

FRENCH GREEN BEANS

A light and elegant side dish that tastes great with any meat.

Makes 6 Servings (V, DF, GF)

 **INGREDIENTS**

 **PREPARATION**

2	12-ounce bags frozen green beans
6	teaspoons Dijon mustard
	Salt and pepper, to taste
4	tablespoons red wine vinegar
6	tablespoons olive oil

1. Cook frozen green beans in the microwave according to package directions.
2. While the beans are cooking, combine mustard, salt and pepper, and mix well.
3. Whisking, add in first the vinegar and then the oil to the mustard until thick.
4. Drizzle mustard vinaigrette on top of cooked beans and mix well until coated.
5. Serve warm or cold.

SPAGHETTI SQUASH NOODLES

Any member of your crew, who is gluten-free, will enjoy spaghetti squash, cooked until tender, then fluffed into delicate, noodle-like strands and served with a sauce of their liking.

Makes 2 to 3 Servings (V, DF, GF)

 ### INGREDIENTS

1   spaghetti squash, whole

 ### PREPARATION

1. Fill a soup pot with 1 inch of water, and place whole squash in it. Cover and bring to a boil over high heat. Cook for 30 minutes, turning once or twice, until squash is tender when pierced with the tip of a knife.
2. Remove the squash, and let it cool. Cut the squash in half lengthwise; remove and discard the seeds with a spoon.
3. Scrape the inside of the squash with a fork, shredding it into noodle-like strands and placing them onto plates or a serving bowl.
4. Top with your favorite sauce.

MEDITERRANEAN SALAD

Each bite is a refreshing blend of juicy, savory, and tangy flavors that feel perfectly in tune with the sunny surroundings.

Makes 6 Servings (V-a, VGT, GF)

 NEVENA MRDALJ

INGREDIENTS

1	cucumber, chopped		1	3-ounce can black olives, sliced
1	pint cherry or grape tomatoes, halved		4	ounces feta cheese crumbles (optional)
½	red onion, sliced		2	tablespoons red wine vinegar
2	green onions, sliced (optional)		3	tablespoons oil

PREPARATION

1. Combine the cucumber, tomatoes, onions and olives, and toss gently with the salad dressing (the combined vinegar and oil).
2. Top with feta cheese, if desired, and serve immediately.

SPINACH WITH BOURSIN

This dish pairs well with steak, grilled chicken or fish, bringing a comforting but light creaminess to balance the meal.

Makes 6 Servings (VGT, GF)

 NEVENA MRDALJ

 **INGREDIENTS**

2	12-ounce bags of frozen chopped spinach	1	5-ounce package Boursin cheese

 **PREPARATION**

1. Cook spinach in the microwave according to package directions. Drain excess water.
2. Put into a serving bowl.
3. Add Boursin cheese, mix well and serve warm.

GRILLED VEGGIES

A colorful mix of vegetables with a touch of charred, smoky flavor that tastes just right.

Makes 6 Servings (V, DF, GF)

NEVENA MRDALJ

 **INGREDIENTS**

Vegetables:

3	large carrots
3	zucchinis
1	green bell pepper
1	red bell pepper
1	yellow bell pepper
	Olive oil, vegetable oil, or nonstick cooking spray

Salt and pepper

Balsamic Dressing:

2	garlic cloves, minced
½	teaspoon salt
4	tablespoons balsamic vinegar
	Dash Italian seasoning mix

 **PREPARATION**

1. Preheat the grill to medium heat.
2. Wash vegetables, pat them dry with a paper towel, and cut them lengthwise into ¼-inch-thick slices. You want them big enough so they don't slip through the grill grates.
3. Brush or spray with oil on all sides.
4. Season with salt and pepper.
5. Grill over direct medium heat until the vegetables are marked and tender:
   Peppers 3 to 4 minutes per side
   Zucchini 4 to 5 minutes per side
   Carrots 5 to 7 minutes per side
6. While vegetables are grilling, mix all the ingredients for the dressing.
7. Once vegetables are done, pour the dressing over grilled vegetables and let sit for 20 minutes, allowing the flavors to blend.
8. Marinated grilled vegetables will keep in the refrigerator for 3 to 4 days.

CHAPTER 14

SWEET ENDINGS

It wouldn't be a vacation without some sweets and desserts. When thinking about dessert items, remember that chocolate bars can be easily brought from home or bought locally; most likely you will need to keep them in the refrigerator if you are not running the air conditioner during the day, but they are compact. Pudding cups come in snack size and are stable at cabin temperature; refrigerate before serving to chill them. There are many popular American cookie varieties in island stores, such as Oreo, Pepperidge Farm, etc. You can find cupcakes, brownies, and freshly baked cookies in bakeries and stores. Some other recipes incorporating local flavors to satisfy a sweet tooth are listed here.

AVOCADO CHOCOLATE MOUSSE

A silky, creamy mousse that is both decadent and nourishing. A satisfying finish to a dinner under the stars.

Makes 6 servings (V, DF, GF)

 **INGREDIENTS**

 **PREPARATION**

4	Hass avocadoes, ripe flesh removed
⅔	cup unsweetened cocoa powder
½	cup honey
1	cup nondairy milk
3	teaspoons vanilla extract
	Nondairy whip cream (optional)

1. Put the first five ingredients into a blender, and blend until smooth. Add more milk if too thick.
2. Refrigerate and serve with whipped cream.

NEVENA MRDALJ

PINEAPPLE CHIA PUDDING

This blend of tropical sweetness and refreshing lightness is an ideal treat for a day at sea.

Makes 6 Servings (V, DF, GF)

 **INGREDIENTS**

1	cup full-fat coconut milk
1	cup almond milk
8	tablespoons chia seeds
4	tablespoons coconut flakes
4	teaspoons sugar
1	cup canned, diced pineapple chunks
3	teaspoons chopped nuts for topping (optional)
3	teaspoons coconut flakes for topping (optional)

 **PREPARATION**

1. Place all ingredients minus the toppings in a small bowl, and mix well until combined.
2. Refrigerate for 1 hour or more.
3. Divide into 6 cups or glasses and garnish with chopped nuts or coconut flakes.

COOL APPLE COMPOTE

Served chilled, this apple compote offers a cool, crisp contrast to the warm
Caribbean breeze.

Makes 6 Servings (V, DF, GF)

NEVENA MRDALJ

INGREDIENTS

6	medium apples	1	teaspoon granola (optional)
½	cup raisins, dried cherries, dried cranberries, or Craisins	1	teaspoon canned whipped cream (optional)
½	lemon, thinly sliced	1	teaspoon rum (optional)
½	teaspoon cinnamon		

PREPARATION

1. Peel and core apples, then cut into chunks.
2. Put the dried fruit and lemon slices in the bottom of a saucepan. Add apple chunks and cinnamon. Add just enough water to barely cover the apples. Bring the water to a boil, and then lower the heat to let the apples simmer for 15 to 20 minutes or until soft, stirring gently once or twice.
3. Remove from heat, and let cool completely.
4. Refrigerate for one to two hours before serving. It will keep in the refrigerator for several days.
5. Serve plain or with a sprinkle of granola, a dollop of whipped cream, or a teaspoon of rum.

MANGO MOUSSE

A luxurious treat that captures the essence of the Caribbean—light, refreshing, and bursting with flavor.

Makes 6 Servings (VGT, V-a)

NEVENA MRDALJ

 **INGREDIENTS**

12	tablespoons sugar		12	tablespoons of canned whipped cream or nondairy whipped topping
6	cups frozen mango chunks			
12	tablespoons fresh lime juice from 3 to 4 limes		6	teaspoons of whipped topping, for garnish
			6	slices of lime, for garnish

 **PREPARATION**

1. Put sugar in the blender, and pulse a few times to pulverize it.
2. Add frozen mango chunks and lime juice, and puree until you have a smooth consistency.
3. Fold in whipping cream gently by hand until smoothly mixed in.
4. Pour into 8-ounce cups, and put the cups in the freezer for at least 1 hour.
5. Take the mousse out 10 minutes before serving.
6. Garnish with an additional dollop of whipped cream and a slice of lime.

COCONUT CHOCOLATE PUDDING

An indulgent and guilt-free treat with a rich chocolate flavor, very light, just like the ocean breeze at night.

Makes 6 servings (V, DF, GF)

INGREDIENTS

6	bananas, fresh or frozen and partially thawed	1½	teaspoons sugar
2	cups coconut milk	2	tablespoons coconut flakes, divided
1	cup cocoa powder		

PREPARATION

1. Combine all ingredients except for one tablespoon of the coconut flakes in the blender and blend until smooth.
2. Refrigerate for at least 1 hour or up to 2 days.
3. Pour into serving glasses and top with the remaining coconut flakes.

GRILLED PINEAPPLE

The pineapple has a bright, natural sweetness - its color mimicking the sun's as it begins to set.

Makes 6 Servings (V, DF, GF)

INGREDIENTS

1   whole ripe pineapple

Olive oil, vegetable oil, or nonstick cooking spray

Sprinkle of salt

Dash of cinnamon (optional)

Dairy-free whipped cream (optional)

PREPARATION

1. Preheat the grill to medium heat.
2. Cut off the top and bottom of the pineapple and remove the outer skin. Cut into ¾-inch-thick slices.
3. Brush or spray both sides lightly with oil.
4. Sprinkle lightly with salt, which will bring out the sweetness of the pineapple.
5. Grill the pineapple slices over direct medium heat for 4 to 5 minutes on each side until caramelized and grill marks appear.
6. Serve with a dash of cinnamon and whipped cream.

NEVENA MRDALJ

READY, SET, SAIL!

Charter yacht vacations are growing in popularity—and with good reason. You will be sharing a beautiful boat with your friends or family members, sailing and cruising from one tropical island to another. However, there are many things to take into consideration when planning a charter yacht vacation with a group. You need to manage expectations regarding food, accommodations, activities, and budget. The better you know everyone, the better you will be able to prepare.

Everyone in the charter industry knows that food is a very important part of the charter yacht experience. According to one blog entitled "Tips on Stocking a Bareboat Charter" (Sailing Tips, October 28, 2021), "Provisioning is part math and part art form, and it takes planning to get it right." Yes, preparation can be very time-consuming, but it is also very doable. Even after more than twenty trips, I follow the steps I have outlined in this book because each trip is unique and so requires planning.

Start planning early and let the excitement build. Make it fun. I encourage you to try some of these recipes at home. If nothing else, you may add a new dish to your weeknight dinner table or for your next dinner party. Almost all the recipes I share in this book I have been preparing for my family for years. As a working mom, I was always looking for quick, easy, and healthy meals. This selection of recipes is well-tested and well-suited for cooking on charter yachts—as I have learned over the past decade.

Actively participating in the planning process, preparing meals together, taking in the beautiful panoramic views while enjoying the ocean breeze—all these experiences will foster connection and make even a simple meal on a boat a time for bonding and joy. As you will soon see, it may take you a few days to get into the rhythm of yacht living, but once you relax and lean into it, it will hopefully be one of your most memorable vacations. You may just get hooked and, like us, keep returning year after year.

See you in paradise and smooth sailing!

APPENDIX

Conversions and Equivalents

Liquid Measurements

Liquid Cooking Measurements

1	cup	8	fluid ounces	16	tablespoons	48	teaspoons	240 ml
½	cup	4	fluid ounces	8	tablespoons	24	teaspoons	120 ml
⅓	cup	2.8	fluid ounces	5.3	tablespoons	16	teaspoons	80 ml
¼	cup	2	fluid ounces	4	tablespoons	12	teaspoons	60 ml
⅛	cup	1	fluid ounces	2	tablespoons	6	teaspoons	30 ml
		0.5	fluid ounces	1	tablespoon	3	teaspoons	15 ml

Beverage Measurements

1	gallon	4	quarts	16	cups	128 fluid ounces	3.8 liters
		1	quart	4	cups	32 fluid ounces	946 ml

Common liquids used in this book:

2 tablespoons oil = 1 fluid ounces = 30 ml

½ cup of mayonnaise = 8 tablespoons

1 chilled milk/juice carton = 1.84 quarts = 59 fluid ounces = 7.5 cups = 1.74 liters

1 UHT milk/ juice carton = 1 quart = 32 fluid ounces = 4 cups = 946 ml

1 gallon = 8 pints = 8 water bottles (16 ounces each)

Weights

Weights

2	ounces	⅛ pound	¼ cup	57 g
4	ounces	¼ pound	½ cup	115 g
8	ounces	½ pound	1 cup	227 g
16	ounces	1 pound	2 cups	455 g

Common weights used in this book:

1 serving of cheese = 1–2 ounces = 1–2 slices

1 serving of lunchmeat = 2–4 ounces = 3–6 slices

Equivalents

These are approximations, but they work well for the recipes present-ed in this guide in Part Two (page 71).

1	tablespoon fresh herbs	1	teaspoon dried
1	tablespoon fresh herbs	½	teaspoon crushed
1	tablespoon fresh herbs	⅓	teaspoon powdered
2	medium cloves of garlic	2	teaspoons minced garlic
2	medium cloves of garlic	¼	teaspoon of garlic powder
1	cup chopped yellow onion	1	medium onion
½	cup chopped green onion	3	green onion stalks
1	cup chopped celery	2	celery stalks
1	cup chopped carrots	2	medium carrots
1	cup cubed cucumber	1	medium cucumber
1	cup cubed cucumber	½	English cucumber
1	cup diced bell peppers	1	medium bell pepper

Common Package Sizes and Number of Servings

- 30-ounce jar of mayonnaise = 60 tablespoons = 40 to 60 servings
- 20-ounce squeezable jar of mayonnaise = 40 tablespoons = 30 to 40 servings
- 24-ounce jar of pickle slices = 8 to 13 servings
- 32-ounce jar of whole pickles = 15 to 20 servings
- 12-ounce jar of cocktail sauce = 6 servings
- 20-ounce bottle of ketchup = 33 servings
- 8-ounce jar of Dijon mustard = 30 to 45 servings
- 22-ounce can of baked beans = 2 to 3.5 servings
- 14-ounce can of diced tomatoes = 3 to 5 servings
- 15-ounce can of whole kernel corn = 2 to 3.5 servings
- 16-ounce jar of peanut butter = 14 servings
- 5-ounce can of tuna = 1 serving
- 24-ounce jar of pasta sauce = 5-6 servings
- 16-ounce bottle of vinegar = 33 tablespoons = 33 servings
- 25-ounce bottle of oil = 50 tablespoons = 50 servings
- 1 pound of cheese = 16-22 slices = 5-10 servings
- 1 pound of lunchmeat =24 slices = 4-8 servings

Checklists and Notes

Boat Briefing

Generator required for:	
a.	
b.	
c.	
d.	
In working order:	
Refrigerator	
Freezer	
Stove or cooktop	
Oven	
Microwave Oven	
Coffee Maker – coffee filters?	
Blender	
Toaster	
Grill	
First Aid Kit—complete?	
Ice Chest Coolers—how many?	
Fire Extinguishers—how many and where?	

Notes:

Essential Dishes and Utensils

	How many?
Serving:	
Dinner Plates	
Salad Plates	
Bowls	
Forks	
Knives	
Spoons, large	
Spoons, small	
Steak knives	
Coffee mugs	
Beverage glasses	
Wine glasses	
Beer and wine bottle opener	
Water pitcher	
Cooking:	
Stockpot	
Pot, small	
Frying pan, large	
Frying pan, small	
Casserole glass dish	
Kitchen knives	
BBQ utensils	
Kitchen scissors	
Cutting board	
Can opener	
Measuring cups	
Measuring spoons	
Large serving bowls (3-4 quarts) with lids	
Pasta strainer	
Pasta scoop	
Peeler	
Ladle	
Spatulas	
Serving spoons	
Serving fork	
Tongs	
Whisk	
Wooden spoons	
Potholders/mitts	
Kitchen towels	

Notes:

The Big Dog

ACKNOWLEDGMENTS

Many latitudes of gratitude to all the following people for their encouragement, support, expertise and inspiration:

My husband, Stevan—my main recipe taster for the past 40 years—whose patience and willingness to wait (sometimes far too long) while I captured the perfect shot of our meals for this book has been nothing short of heroic. From countless taste tests to unforgettable boat adventures, we've shared incredible memories—both on land and at sea!

My daughter, Maja, who had the difficult task of reading my first draft and gave me great advice on which recipes to include, what to leave out, and how to organize this guide.

My son, Nik, who was my beta reader and gave me invaluable feedback.

Our local charter yacht experts in the British Virgin Islands, Clarence Malone and Fayola Browne, for encouraging me to write this book because charterers would find it helpful.

My friend, Tama, who cheered me on from the start and who told me to stick with this creative process and to stay true to my own vision.

My editor, Katie Benoit, whose editorial expertise helped me to organize and develop my ideas, my copious notes, and all the recipes into an actual book.

My photo advisor and mentor, Janise, who helped me select my best photos and told me how to take better ones.

My neighbor, Greg Brown, who held an educational workshop on writing books and made it sound possible.

My friend, Kim Dwyer, an experienced sailor whose feedback early on was very helpful.

David Powdrell, a professional photographer whom I met very briefly in the British Virgin Islands, but whose encouragement made a big impact on me.

Rob Bignell, who proofread the final manuscript and helped with other aspects of this project.

All the people in the Virgin Islands and elsewhere, who work so hard, always with a friendly smile on their face, to make our vacations enjoyable.

Our friends and family members with whom we have shared many memorable moments.

A big thank you to all of you from the bottom of my heart,
NEVENA

ABOUT THE AUTHOR

Nevena Mrdalj is a seasoned charter yacht traveler with over a decade of experience in provisioning, meal planning, and cooking aboard bareboat charters. From the Virgin Islands and Puerto Rico to the Bahamas, Canada, and the South of France, she has perfected the art of preparing simple, delicious, and boat-friendly meals—all while navigating the unique challenges of provisioning at sea.

A working mom with a passion for creating quick, easy, and healthy meals, Nevena has spent years refining a collection of tried-and-true recipes that work just as well for busy weeknights as they do for a week-long yacht vacation. What began as a personal mission to streamline provisioning—after an unforgettable (and somewhat chaotic) first charter trip—evolved into this guide, packed with practical tips, adaptable meal plans for various dietary needs, and foolproof recipes for stress-free meals on the water.

Whether you're a first-time charterer or a seasoned sailor, Nevena's insights will help you set sail with confidence and enjoy every meal along the way.

When not sailing or planning her next adventure, Nevena loves entertaining, spending time with family, reading, and photography. She and her husband live in Tucson, AZ.

Learn more at **SetSailCookbook.com.**
Instagram: @setsailcookbook
Facebook: setsailcookbook